HOW THINGS ARE MADE

■ BOOKS FOR WORLD EXPLORERS
NATIONAL GEOGRAPHIC SOCIETY

Ironworkers build supports for a bridge over San Francisco Bay, in California.

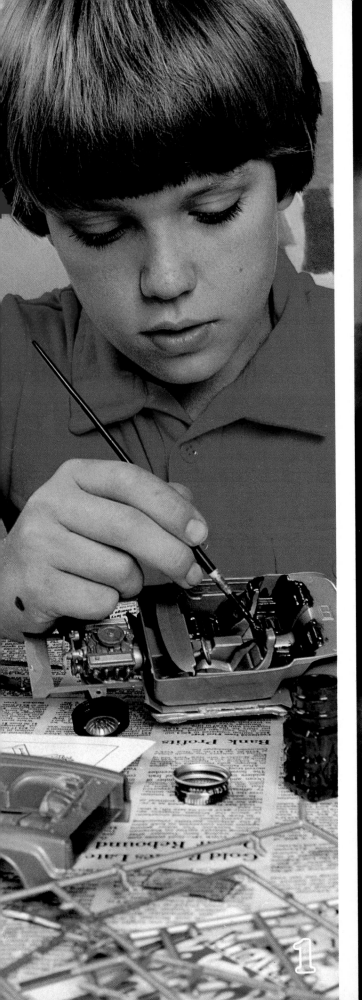

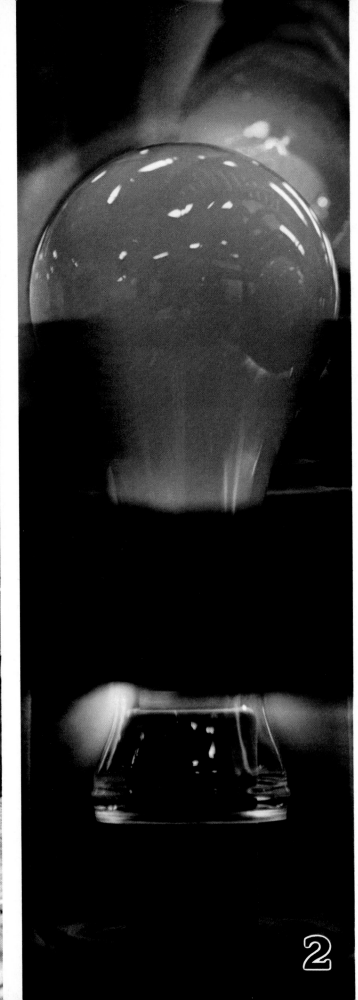

CONTENTS

COPYRIGHT © 1981
NATIONAL GEOGRAPHIC SOCIETY
LIBRARY OF CONGRESS CIP DATA: PAGE 103

*COVER: Boeing 747 jumbo jet nears
completion in Everett, Washington.*
THE BOEING COMPANY

MANUFACTURING THROUGH THE AGES

We use them every day—the countless "things" that surround us. Paper, light bulbs, clocks, toothpaste—they're all a part of our lives. You could probably make a long list of things you've used just today. But do you know how any of those things were made?

For centuries, people had to make every item by hand. Some things are still made that way. But over the years, other ways of making and assembling products have been developed. Machines have been invented that can make some things quickly and inexpensively.

Most of the changes in the ways people make things have taken place in the last 200 years. The drawings here and on the next three pages show four of the most important of these changes: the division of labor, the use of machines to build products, the manufacture of things with interchangeable parts, and the introduction of the assembly line.

People at work in a pinmaking factory

1. Unreeling brass wire for pins

2. Cutting the wire to the proper length

3. Sharpening the pins

A craftsman making a pin

◀ Story With a Point

Long ago, craftsmen made their products by hand, one at a time. Often, a single craftsman made a product from start to finish. The common straight pin, for example, was once made this way. A pinmaker first hammered the shaft of a pin out of a piece of metal. Then the craftsman shaped one end to form the head and sharpened the other end to form the point. Making pins this way was very slow. And each handmade pin was usually different from all others.

4. Adding the heads

5. Coating the pins with tin

6. Packing the finished pins

▼ From People to Machines

Dividing pinmaking into separate steps gave some inventors of machines an idea. The inventors realized that a machine could be built to do each of the same simple steps that human pinmakers performed. In 1832, an American named John Ireland Howe built a pinmaking machine that worked well. All the pins made by the Howe machine were just alike, and they were cheaper to make than handmade pins. However, Howe's machine could not use metal that was as hard as the metal used by human pinmakers. As a result, the machine-made pins were more likely to bend. When people compared machine-made pins with handmade pins, they saw that the machine-made versions had both advantages and disadvantages. This is true of many products made by machines.

The Howe pinmaking machine in operation

▲ Dividing the Work

By the late 1700s, craftsmen had begun assigning a different person to perform each of the steps in pinmaking. When the work was divided this way, as many as 18 persons helped make a single pin. Each worker soon became skilled in performing his own particular task. As a result, the pins the workers made were more nearly alike. A group of workers could make a pin faster than a single person working alone could. Because of this, the cost of the pins went down. Using different workers to perform different steps is called the division of labor.

▼ Parts That Are Alike

In the first half of the 1800s, the United States government encouraged the development of muskets and rifles with interchangeable parts. An interchangeable part is one that is exactly like all other parts made for the same purpose. If parts are alike, one can be substituted for another. Muskets with interchangeable parts could be assembled much faster than muskets with parts that were not alike. For example, a gunmaker could take any trigger from a pile of interchangeable triggers and the part would fit exactly into place. Muskets with interchangeable parts were also easier to repair, because broken parts could be replaced quickly.

A worker assembling a musket from interchangeable parts

1. Completing engines

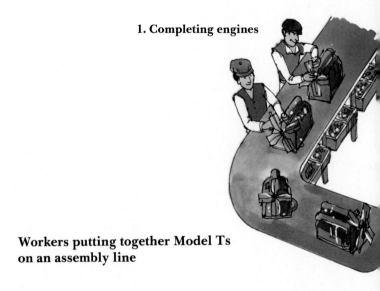

Workers putting together Model Ts on an assembly line

2. Attaching gas tanks to frames

Mr. Ford and His Model T ▲

In the early 1900s, Henry Ford and his engineers at the Ford Motor Company worked out a new method of assembling the thousands of inter-changeable parts that made up the Model T automobile. Ford decided not to assemble this car by bringing all the parts and all the workers together in one spot. Instead, he brought the parts to workers who were spread out in long lines. Each worker performed only a small job as one Model T after another moved slowly by. The long lines where the cars were put together piece by piece came to be called assembly lines. Today,

6

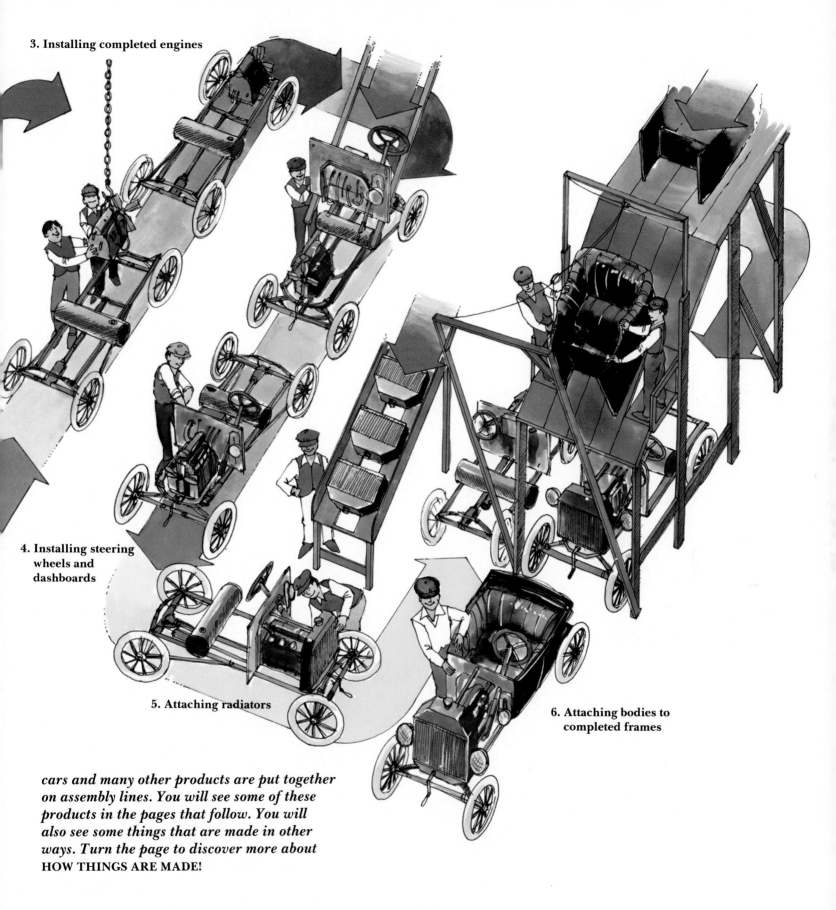

3. Installing completed engines

4. Installing steering wheels and dashboards

5. Attaching radiators

6. Attaching bodies to completed frames

cars and many other products are put together on assembly lines. You will see some of these products in the pages that follow. You will also see some things that are made in other ways. Turn the page to discover more about **HOW THINGS ARE MADE!**

1
HOW FUN THINGS ARE MADE

Touch of Color

Jason Otto, 10, of Venice, California, paints the seats of a model car. Jason is putting the model together from a kit. To see how model kits are made, turn the page.

LIANE ENKELIS

Balls, bicycles, and blocks . . . dolls, puzzles, and kites . . . tops, models, and computer football games. Our lives are filled with fun things like these. Making objects that are meant to entertain us is nothing new. People have made and used fun things for thousands of years. Archaeologists—scientists who study the past—have found dolls, toy wagons, and other playthings in ruins of old cities. These scientists have discovered that Egyptians played board games 5,000 years ago. And they've learned that people in ancient Rome sometimes played with tops.

Board games and tops still provide fun for people. What is it that makes these and other objects fun to use? Part of the explanation is the power of the imagination. If you use your imagination, a corncob wrapped in cloth can become a doll. A row of chairs can turn into a train. Imagination also makes the objects we buy in stores more fun to play with. The model airplane you build can take part in battles—or even fly off into space—if you use your imagination.

But there is more than just fun to fun things. These objects can encourage us to use our physical and mental abilities in new ways. They may challenge us to ride a bicycle faster than we ever have ridden before, to skate more gracefully, or to play checkers with greater skill.

On the pages that follow, you will find out how several kinds of fun things are made. You will learn what creates the colorful patterns inside a kaleidoscope. You will find out how a root from a leafy plant flavors something good to eat. And you will see what a stuffed animal looks like before it is stuffed.

PLASTIC MODELS

You have to pay attention to details when you assemble a plastic model. And so do the people who make model kits. Revell, Inc., of Venice, California, produces about ten million kits a year. Some have more than a hundred parts.

Model kits available today include almost every kind of vehicle, from sailing ships to space shuttles. Kit manufacturers try to make sure their models are accurate down to the tiniest detail. To create a new model car, for example, Revell researchers may obtain blueprints from the car manufacturer. Or the researchers may photograph and measure an actual car.

The researchers give this information to Revell's engineers. The engineers use the information to draw detailed plans of the model car. The plans show how the model will look both before and after it is put together.

The plans are then used to make patterns from which a steel mold is later made. Melted plastic forced into the mold produces the finished parts that go into the kit.

From Big to Small *To outline the shape of a car, Douglas Walker guides one end of a device called a pantograph along taped lines. A pencil on the other end draws the shape of the car on paper in a reduced size.*

10

Shaping Clay

Allan Erickson smooths clay over a wood and plastic form. He is shaping a rough model of a car. Erickson made the form by copying the outline of the car from plans based on pantograph drawings. Plaster will be poured over the model to make a mold. The plaster mold will be used to produce additional patterns from which the final steel mold will be made.

Cutting Steel

John Curwen (left) uses a small pantograph to transfer the outline of a model car from a hard plastic pattern to a steel mold. A sharp blade cuts the car's outline into the steel. Below, Jack White puts the finishing touches on the two halves of a steel mold. He uses a pencil-size grinder. Tiny details, such as hood ornaments and door handles, have been engraved in the mold by hand. Turn the page to see a mold in use.

LIANE ENKELIS (ALL)

Molding Plastic

The open jaws of a molding machine (below) show the parts of a just-produced plastic model inside. Melted plastic filled the mold to produce these parts. The hot plastic cooled and hardened in seconds. One molding machine can produce about 200 such models each hour.

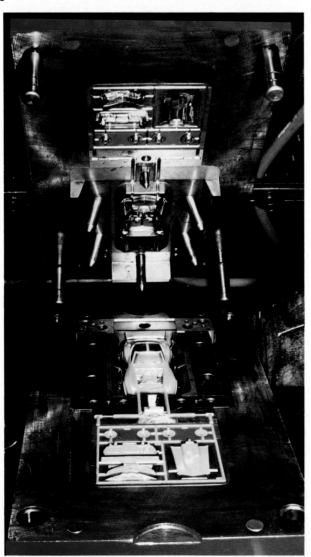

LIANE ENKELIS (ALL)

Instant 'Chrome'

Archie James (above) hangs tiny aluminum rods inside a machine that produces a chrome-like finish on plastic parts. Air inside the machine is pumped out, creating a vacuum. The tiny pieces of aluminum are then heated by electricity until they vaporize. In the vacuum, the aluminum coats all the plastic parts evenly. The result—instant "chrome"—is shown on the opposite page. After the plastic parts of a model are complete, they are packaged along with decals and instruction sheets. The kits are then ready for shipment.

12

BICYCLES

Today's bicycles look quite different from earlier versions. One early two-wheeled vehicle, called a hobby horse, had a wooden frame. Invented in Europe about 1816, hobby horses had no pedals. Riders propelled them by pushing against the ground with their feet.

About 1840, a Scottish blacksmith developed a bicycle with pedals attached to the rear wheel by metal rods. This idea did not catch on. Other inventors began to experiment with putting pedals on the front wheel. Gradually, the front wheels of bicycles became larger, and the rear wheels became smaller.

A large front wheel was designed to increase the bike's speed. The bigger the front wheel was, the farther—and faster—one turn of the pedals would make the bike go. Some of these bicycles had front wheels five feet (152 cm)* high. People often were injured by falling off these tall bikes.

In the 1880s, inventors in England designed a bicycle with two smaller wheels of nearly equal size. The rider sat between the wheels, pumping pedals attached to the rear wheel by a chain. This bicycle became known as the safety bike because it was safer to ride than the kind with a large front wheel. The safety bike set the pattern for the modern bicycle.

Two-wheeled Fun

Kate Marsh, left, and Jonna Berman, both 14, enjoy a bicycle ride along a sidewalk in their hometown of Wilmette, Illinois (left).

Colorful Job

An overhead conveyor carries painted chain guards (right). Painted parts get one undercoat and one or two finish coats. Bikes with metallic finishes get a coat of aluminum paint before the final color is added. Between each coat, parts dry in an oven for about half an hour. Turn the page to see how bikes are assembled.

*Metric figures in this book are given in round numbers.

IRA BLOCK (ALL)

Frame Up

At the Schwinn Bicycle Company, in Chicago, Illinois, a worker joins steel tubes together to form a bicycle frame. When the frame is complete, it will be cleaned and painted.

15

Racks of Rims

Workers check newly chrome-plated wheel rims for defects. Behind them, rims emerge from a cleaning vat after being plated. Rims are pressed from strips of steel, then welded to form rings.

Adding Spokes

Skilled hands attach spokes to a hub (right). The other ends of the spokes will be attached to the rim. The wheel will be straightened, then the tube and tire will be added.

Shift Levers

A steel cable slides into its casing (far right). The cable is fastened at one end to the gearshift levers shown here. The other end is attached to the part that moves the bicycle's chain from gear to gear.

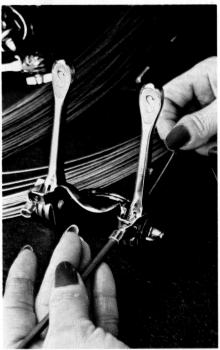

Last-minute Repair

A worker adjusts the rear wheel of a bicycle taken from the assembly line. In this part of the factory, wheels, brakes, and other parts are added as the bicycles move slowly past the workers.

Ready for Shipping

Inspectors check bicycles near the end of the assembly line (below). The bikes are then packed for delivery. To save shipping space, bicycles are boxed without pedals, handlebars, or seats in place. Dealers attach these parts.

KALEIDOSCOPES

Look inside a kaleidoscope and you'll see a beautiful pattern of colors. If you turn the kaleidoscope, you'll see a new pattern. A Scottish scientist invented this toy in 1816. He put bits of colored glass in a long tube. He also put two mirrors inside. When the tube was turned, the glass bits tumbled around. The mirrors reflected and multiplied each pattern made by the bits of glass. Although the kaleidoscope is a toy, designers of carpets, wallpaper, and fabrics have used it to get ideas for new patterns.

IRA BLOCK (ALL)

Shiny Shapes

Metal mirrors fit inside cardboard kaleidoscope tubes (above). The mirrors will reflect the plastic chips being added at left. The chips are held between two plastic disks, one inside the tube and the other at one end. The kaleidoscopes are being made at the Steven Manufacturing Company, in Hermann, Missouri.

Rings for Tubes

Linda Walkenbach operates a machine that attaches metal rings to kaleidoscopes. The rings hold the end pieces in place.

One Last Look

John Waters tests completed kaleidoscopes for quality. Rejected kaleidoscopes are returned for repair. Steven Manufacturing makes thousands of these toys each year.

BASEBALLS

A pitcher throws a baseball, and the batter takes a hard swing. Fans hear a loud CRACK, and the ball sails into the outfield for a hit. The baseball the players are using is new. But it was made in nearly the same way baseballs were manufactured more than a hundred years ago.

J. deBeer & Son, Inc., of Albany, New York, made the ball. This company started making baseballs in 1889. It began making softballs in the 1920s. Both types of balls are put together using similar techniques. Since deBeer started making baseballs, its basic methods of manufacture have changed very little.

The best baseballs begin with cork centers that are covered with rubber. Machines wrap layers of yarn around the rubber. Workers dip the wrapped balls in latex glue to hold the yarn in place. A machine cuts the covers for the balls out of leather. Finally, workers sew the covers on the balls by hand.

N.G.S. PHOTOGRAPHER JOSEPH H. BAILEY (BOTH)

Sticky Bath

A worker dips yarn-wrapped balls into a bucket of latex glue. The thin coat of glue that sticks to the balls will help keep the yarn from shifting when the balls are hit with a bat. Turn the page to see how covers are made and sewn on.

What's Inside

Balls wrapped with yarn (left) are ready to be dipped in latex glue. After the balls are dipped, their covers will be sewn on. The diagram above

Parts of a Baseball

A cork center wrapped with black rubber and red rubber gives the ball bounce and produces a cracking sound when the ball is hit.

Layers of wool yarn build up the ball to the correct size.

One layer of cotton yarn gives the wrapped ball a smooth finish.

The hand-stitched cover holds the ball together.

shows the parts of a top-quality baseball. Other kinds of balls contain different materials and are made in different ways.

Stamping Machine

The machine on the left stamps out figure-eight-shaped pieces for covers. To make a cover, two of these pieces will be sewn around a ball by hand.

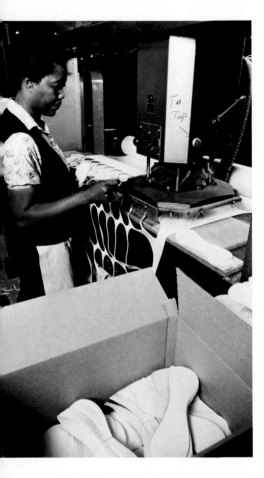

Sewing Room

Workers sew covers on baseballs (below). No machine can make the right stitches. On the average, one person can sew covers on seven balls an hour.

N.G.S. PHOTOGRAPHER JOSEPH H. BAILEY (ALL)

Final Stitches

Two needles stitch together the pieces of a cover. After the ball is sewn, it will be weighed, measured, and inspected. Top-quality baseballs must weigh 5 to 5$\frac{1}{4}$ ounces (142-149 g) and measure 9 to 9$\frac{1}{4}$ inches (about 23 cm) around. Players in Varnell, Georgia (opposite page), use the finished product in a practice game.

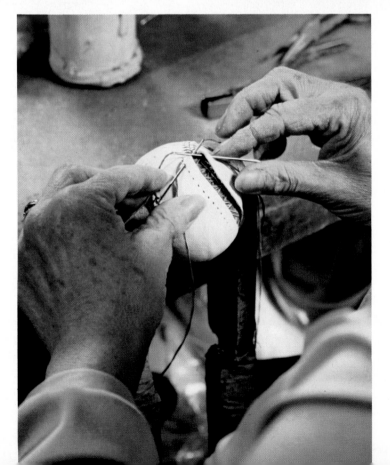

22

LICORICE

You probably would be surprised if a friend offered you some licorice—then handed you a piece of brown root. Yet licorice candy actually is made from such roots. The roots come from the licorice plant, a relative of peas and beans.

Licorice plants grow in parts of southern Europe and the Middle East, and in areas of the U.S.S.R. and the People's Republic of China. Laborers dig up the roots and separate them from the leafy tops. The roots are piled up and left to dry for several months. The dried roots are then tied together and pressed into bales for shipping.

When licorice root arrives in this country, it is first ground and boiled. The boiling liquid absorbs the flavor of the root. This liquid, called extract, is then dried to make a powder that is shipped to candy companies. The photographs here and on the next page show how one company turns the powder into candy.

Lifting Cargo

Workers unload a ship carrying thousands of tons of dried licorice root (right). This shipment came from China. A crane lifts the bales of roots from inside the ship.

Underground Sweet

The roots of the licorice plant (right) are the only parts used in making candy. Licorice roots contain a substance fifty times sweeter than sugar.

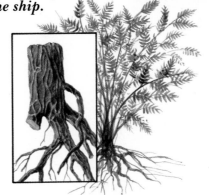

Candy With a Twist

Rotating nozzles on a machine called an extruder (left) add the twist to a fresh batch of licorice. This licorice is being made at Y & S Candies, Inc., in Lancaster, Pennsylvania.

Powder From Roots

Licorice powder (right) will be mixed with other ingredients to make candy.

N.G.S. PHOTOGRAPHER JOSEPH H. BAILEY (ALL)

Mixing Candy

A worker adjusts a chute used to transfer flour and starch from an overhead scale to a mixing tank (left). The flour and starch will be mixed with licorice powder and eight other ingredients. This mixture then will be cooked.

Hot Licorice

Freshly cooked licorice flows from a pipe into the extruder that shapes the candy. This worker makes sure the hot licorice flows into the extruder at the right speed.

Cut and Dried

Candy that has been twisted by the extruder and cut into equal lengths is placed on trays to dry. After it has dried, the candy is packaged in cellophane bags for shipment.

STUFFED ANIMALS

Matching Cloth to Fur   *At a stuffed-animal factory, Laurie Hoffman uses a picture of animals to help her select plush fabric that looks like real fur.*

A monkey sits on a table while someone draws a smile on its face. A lion's eyes sparkle as a worker sews on a shiny nose. These creatures are stuffed animals. They are being made at R. Dakin & Company, in Lindsay, California.

Stuffed animals such as these have been made for many years. America's most popular stuffed animal, the teddy bear, was named for President Theodore (Teddy) Roosevelt. In 1902, the President spared the life of a bear cub while on a hunting trip. When a toy maker heard about this, he made a stuffed bear and called it Teddy's Bear.

R. Dakin & Company makes thousands of stuffed animals every year. To see how the toy known as Big Jocko is made, turn the page.

27

Punching Out Fabric

Robert Tillery (left) positions a metal pattern over the fabric used to make Big Jocko. The orange part of the machine at Tillery's right will push the pattern through the fabric like a giant cookie cutter.

PATTERN © R. DAKIN & COMPANY

LIANE ENKELIS (ALL)

All the Pieces

The pieces needed to make Big Jocko have all been punched out (above). Next, they will be sewn together inside out. This is done so the seams will not show later. After being sewn, the toys are turned right side out.

Feeling Stuffed

Ruben Ramirez operates a machine that blows foam-rubber stuffing through a small hole left in a seam of the toy. The hole will later be sewn shut.

Give Us a Smile

With a felt-tip marker, Adela Zerafin draws eyebrows, nostrils, and a mouth on Big Jocko. Plastic eyes were added when the toy was sewn.

Fuzzy Friends

It's hard to choose a favorite when you can pick from so many different stuffed animals. Cuddling up to Big Jocko and other toys are, from the left, Erin Norris, 9, Diane Lau, 8, and Greg Nomura, 9. All three children live in San Francisco, California.

2

HOW USEFUL THINGS ARE MADE

Can you decide which of the things around your home is the most useful? Is it the furnace or the refrigerator? The garbage disposal or the lawn mower?

Your idea of which item is most useful probably depends on what activity is most important to you. To an artist, a paintbrush is useful. But to someone who never paints, a brush has little value. A plumber uses special tools every day. But most people never need to use such tools at all.

Many useful objects around our homes have been invented within the last century. Things that would have been unimaginable to someone living in the 1800s have become everyday objects to us. Think what people who lived a hundred years ago would say if they could see an automatic dishwasher, a smoke detector, an air conditioner, or a color television set.

You may have heard about the "necessities of life"—food, clothing, and shelter. Many of the things that people make are meant to provide at least one of these necessities. The corn a farmer grows may be made into the cereal you eat for breakfast. Wool sheared from a sheep's body may be woven into a warm coat or sweater. A tree cut down on a hillside may be turned into a floor in your house. Useful products such as these are some of the most important things that people make.

On the following pages, you will see how several useful objects are made. You will learn how toothpaste is mixed and squirted into tubes. You will see a machine that puts together colorful felt-tip markers. And you will watch a blacksmith hammer out a handy fireplace tool.

LIGHT BULBS

Flip a switch and light instantly fills a room. All it takes is a single light bulb. What makes this bulb glow so brightly?

The answer, of course, is electricity. When electricity passes through metal, the metal becomes hot. Inside a light bulb, electricity passes through a fine metal wire called a filament. The electricity makes the filament so hot that it glows with a brilliant white light.

Surrounded by air, the heated filament would soon burn up. To prevent this, the filament is placed inside a glass bulb and the air is drawn out of the bulb. This process protects the filament. The bulb is then sealed, and a metal cap is cemented to its base. Here and on the following pages, you can see how Sylvania light bulbs are made at the GTE Lighting Products factory in Saint Marys, Pennsylvania.

Inside and Out

Light bulb parts (above) surround a completed bulb, center. Clockwise from the bottom: glass tubes and wires that will form a filament unit; a completed filament unit; a clear glass bulb; a bulb that has been coated inside; two clear bulbs with filament units in place; a base cap.

Cutting the Glare

Blue flames (below, left) dry moisture from a clear glass bulb. While still hot, the bulb's inner surface is sprayed with a special coating (below, right). This white coating will make the bulb's light softer.

Molding Filament Mounts

Softened by flames, glass mounts that will hold filaments are molded into shape (above). A machine will later clamp the filaments—lengths of thin, coiled wire—between the pairs of wires that stick from the mounts' glowing orange tips. The orange streak in this picture was caused by the rapid movement of the hot glass mounts.

Protecting Wires

Filaments in their glass mounts (right) are dipped into a mixture called getter. After the filaments are dipped, the mounts will be sealed inside bulbs. Air left in the bulbs will be drawn out. Oxygen in the air can ruin heated filaments. The first time the bulbs are lit, the getter on the filaments will burn away, removing traces of oxygen that are left.

33

Adding Bases

A machine places metal bases on the ends of bulbs (right). The wires leading from the filament are then trimmed and attached to the base. The wires will carry electricity to the filament.

Making a Seal

Burning alcohol flares from a base (left). The cement that holds on the base contains alcohol. When the cement is heated, the alcohol burns away, and the cement hardens.

Fragile Pile

A conveyor belt gently delivers bulbs to a storage box (right). From there, the bulbs will travel to the inspection room. The information printed on these bulbs includes their wattage, or the rate at which they use energy.

Final Test

Eyes shaded from the glare, an inspector checks finished bulbs for flaws (left). The factory where she works produces millions of bulbs each month. Before any bulb leaves the factory, it must pass this test.

TOOTHPASTE

Long ago, a famous Greek doctor had a good idea. The doctor's name was Hippocrates (say Hip-PAH-cruh-teez). He recommended that people clean their teeth with powder made of the stone called marble. Marble is made up of minerals. Today—2,400 years later—most toothpastes still contain powdered minerals.

Toothpastes made today also contain other ingredients, such as water, coloring, and flavoring. Some toothpastes contain a special ingredient called fluoride. Many scientists believe that fluoride helps keep teeth from decaying by hardening the outer part, or enamel, of the teeth.

Brushing your teeth with toothpaste helps remove a film called plaque. Plaque contains germs that can cause cavities and gum disease. The pictures here and on page 38 show how one kind of toothpaste is made.

Mixing Toothpaste

A worker adds powder called cellulose gum to a batch of Aim toothpaste. Aim contains 12 ingredients. Cellulose gum is a binder that helps hold these ingredients together. The worker wears a mask to avoid breathing any powder.

Out of the Carton

Metal lifting rods remove empty tubes from a carton. The rods will place the tubes on a belt that will carry them to the filling machine.

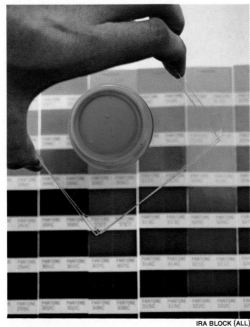

IRA BLOCK (ALL)

Colorful Test

A sample of toothpaste is checked to see if it is the desired shade of blue.

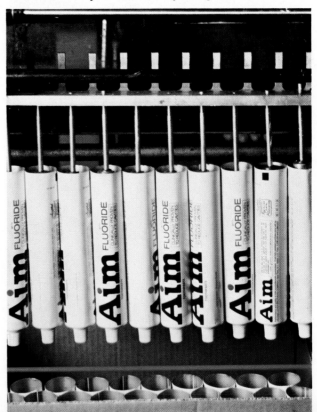

Quality Check

A sample of toothpaste to be tested pours from a valve on the filling machine. Workers check each batch several times to see if the toothpaste is the right color and thickness.

Bottoms Up!

Nozzles on the filling machine squirt toothpaste into the tubes. This machine will then seal the open end of each tube.

IRA BLOCK

Ready for Squeezing

Filled tubes slide into boxes (above). After the machine closes the ends of the boxes, the toothpaste will be ready for shipment. Will Toft (right) is about to brush his teeth. Will, 11, of Arlington, Virginia, tries to prevent cavities by brushing daily.

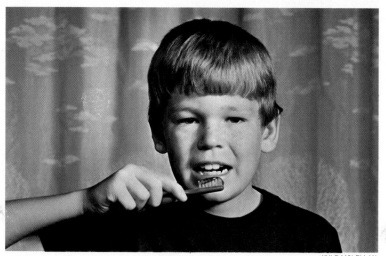

KYLE MCLELLAN

FELT-TIP MARKERS

With a felt-tip marker, you can write your name in bold, wide strokes. Or you can make fine, delicate lines. Inside a felt-tip marker is a wick-like filling soaked with fast-drying ink. The ink flows into the tip of the marker as you write. Felt-tip markers come with many colors of ink. They can be used to write on a variety of materials, including metal, glass, and plastic, as well as paper.

The picture below shows felt-tip markers made by Paper Mate, in Santa Monica, California. First, the separate parts of the markers were manufactured. Then a single machine put all the parts together.

Swirling Samples *Multicolored patterns appear as a machine tests new felt-tip markers. The test shows whether the right amount of ink flows from the tips. Turn the page to see markers being made.*

ALBERT MOLDVAY

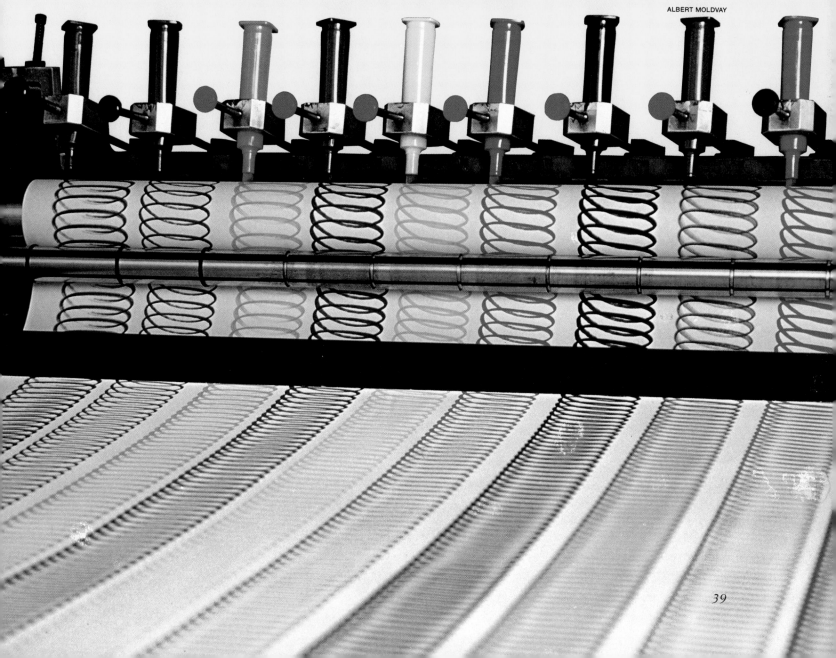

Here's a Tip

Strands of a soft material called polyester (right) feed into a machine that forms marker tips. A worker holds samples of the tips. These will later be trimmed for writing.

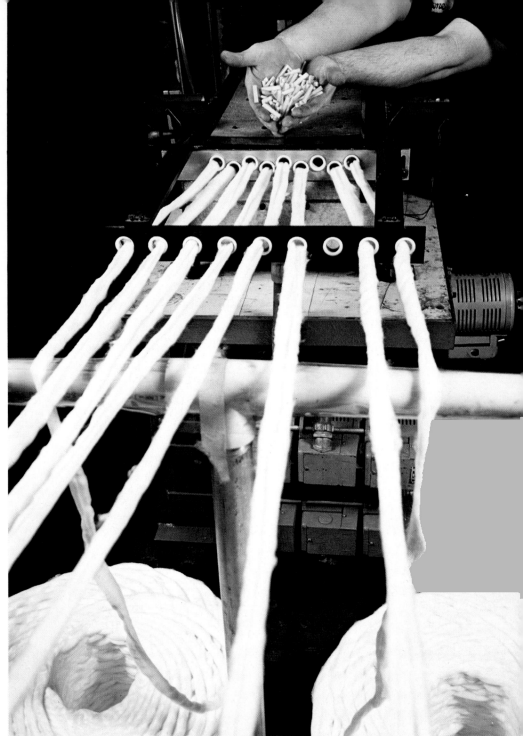

Bits and Pieces

The bits of plastic above will be melted to form marker bodies like the one shown. After such bits are melted, the plastic is forced through a nozzle into a mold. There, it cools and hardens into a marker body. The red bits of plastic provide color and shine. The clear ones make the body strong, yet flexible.

ALBERT MOLDVAY (ALL)

Get the Point

A pen tip flies from a grinding machine. This machine shapes tips to the proper angle for writing. Next, the parts of the markers will be assembled.

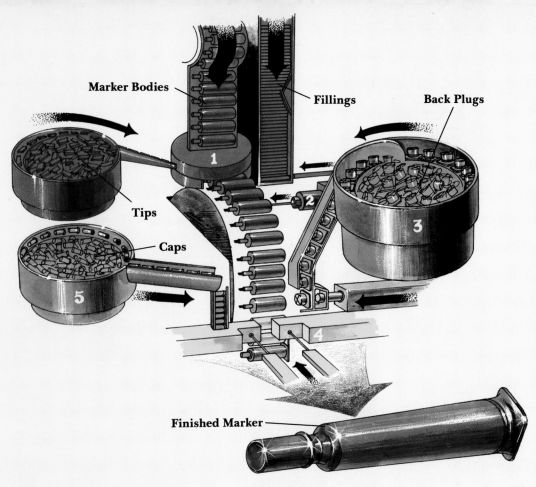

Marker Bodies

Fillings

Back Plugs

Tips

Caps

Finished Marker

Putting It Together

The drawing at left shows a machine stocked with all the parts that go into felt-tip markers. First, a plastic marker body drops into position in the center of the machine. There, the tip and the filling are pushed into the body (1). Next, a needle shoots ink into the filling (2). Then a back plug (3) is attached. Wires pushed through the marker hold the tip and the plug in place (4). The machine then presses on a cap (5). This machine can assemble about 3,500 markers in an hour.

Now You See It, Now You Don't

The gooey substance this woman holds looks like tar. But it is really a special erasable ink used in some pens. Scientists in The Paper Mate Division of The Gillette Company invented it by combining ink with rubber. The erasable ink dries slowly and can be rubbed off before it has hardened (below). After about 24 hours, the ink dries, and the writing becomes permanent.

N.G.S. PHOTOGRAPHER JOSEPH H. BAILEY

FIREPLACE TOOLS

Everyone knows that Superman can bend steel . . . but then, so can blacksmiths! A blacksmith uses special tools to bend the metal. He uses fire to heat and soften iron or steel.

Many years ago, blacksmiths supplied people with a variety of everyday items. They made cooking utensils, tools, plows, and even metal toys. Today, most metal products are made in factories. But not all.

In his shop in Mount Holly, Vermont, blacksmith Pete Taggett and three employees make fireplace tools, candleholders, and other metal items. They make them in the same way that blacksmiths made such things long ago.

Taggett taught himself the skills of the blacksmith in 1971. At first, his shop was a one-man operation. But word about his work soon spread. Business began to grow. Today, Taggett sells his products in all fifty states.

Shaping Cold Steel

Steve Duprey bends a steel rod that will be made into a fireplace tool. Steve, 18, uses a shaping device to bend the steel. The device helps him put the bend in exactly the right place.

CLAYTON J. PRICE (ALL)

Preparing the Fire

Blacksmith Pete Taggett prepares a coal fire that will be used to heat the rod Steve has bent. The metal must be heated before it can be shaped further.

Heart of a Blacksmith Shop

The blacksmith's forge is the most important piece of equipment in the shop. The forge provides heat needed to soften metal so it can be shaped more easily. To produce a very hot fire, air is forced through burning coals. By turning a knob, the blacksmith controls the amount of air forced through the coals. This regulates the heat level.

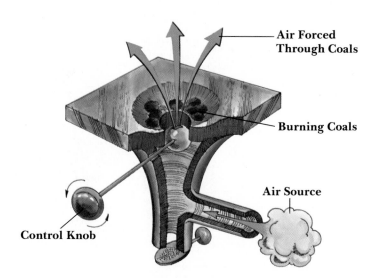

Air Forced Through Coals

Burning Coals

Air Source

Control Knob

42

...een heated, William Lienhard clamps it in a vise. Shaping hot iron or steel is called forging. With the rod held securely, Lienhard will twist it into a decorative shape.

Hammering the Steel

Lienhard straightens the handle of the fireplace tool after the twist has been added (below). He uses a hammer and an anvil. When the handle is straight, Lienhard will dunk it in water. The water will cool and harden the steel.

Handling Hot Metal

Lienhard twists the rod using a blacksmith's tool called a tee handle. He can work with hot steel only for about thirty seconds at a time. If an operation takes longer, Lienhard must reheat the metal to keep it soft enough to shape.

Adding a Bend

Peter Walczuk forges the opposite end of the fireplace tool into a poker (above). Finished pokers rest in the bucket to his right.

Finished Tool Set

A completed set of handmade tools sits ready for shipment (right). The blacksmiths used 14 pieces of steel and went through 65 steps to produce these tools. The set sells for about $75.

WOOL CLOTH

Many kinds of animals have coats of wool. Wool is made up of hairlike fibers that have a waxy coating called wool grease. The grease makes the animals' coats water-resistant.

Thousands of years ago, people discovered that they could make warm clothing from the hides and wool of sheep. Later, people learned how to shear sheep and weave the wool into cloth on looms. Natural waves in wool fibers, called crimps, allow the fibers to be twisted and stretched into yarn without being damaged.

Today, giant looms in some woolen mills weave huge sheets of cloth nearly 200 feet (60 m) long. The pictures below and those on the following pages show how wool is made into yarn and how the yarn is woven into cloth at the Pendleton Woolen Mills plant in Washougal, Washington.

Sheep Shearing

Oregon farmer Lynn Trupp (left) finishes shearing a sheep. Shearing the animal does not hurt it. This sheep produces up to 20 pounds (9 kg) of wool yearly. Its wool is made into cloth.

Fuzzy Samples

Raw wool fibers (above) range in texture from coarse to fine. Different types of wool are mixed to produce the proper blend for making yarn.

Adding Color

Bill Bellwood (right) stirs wool fibers inside a dyeing vat to ensure an even color. Red dye flows up through the column in the center of the vat. The dye then sprays over the wool.

JEFF BECKER (ALL)

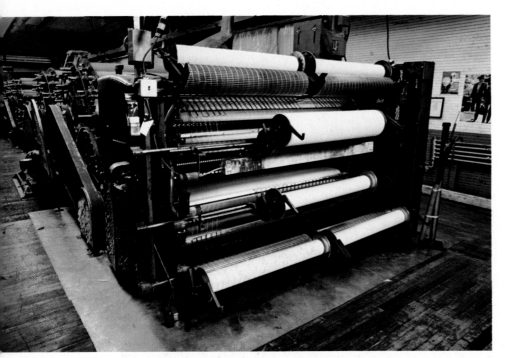

Producing Roving

Here is what happens inside a carding machine: Clumps of wool pass between many sets of wire-covered rollers, like the set in the drawing below. The rollers break up the clumps and straighten the fibers. The rollers then comb the fibers until they form a thin web. Later, smooth rollers will divide the web and press it into fine strands of roving.

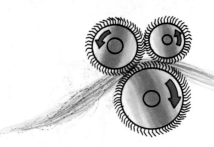

Separating Fibers

A carding machine (above) straightens wool fibers and separates them into fine strands called roving.

Spinning Yarn

Yarn that has been spun from roving winds onto bobbins as it comes from a spinning machine (left). Audrey Browning checks the bobbins to see if they are full. The spinning machine twists the fine strands of wool, giving them added strength. The yarn produced is later steamed to make the twist permanent. Steaming also reduces kinking during weaving. The yarn above is ready to be woven into cloth.

Preparing Yarn

Hilda Bellwood (above) runs a machine that winds long strands of yarn so they will produce the correct color pattern on a loom.

Weaving Cloth on a Loom

Many long strands of yarn run from end to end on a loom (below). More yarn is wound inside a device called a shuttle. The shuttle passes from one side of the loom to the other, weaving yarn between the long strands. Two frames called harnesses separate the long strands by raising every other one. When the shuttle moves in one direction, yarn passes above the first long strand, then below the next, and so on. Just before the shuttle moves in the other direction, the harnesses reverse the positions of the long strands. The yarn from the shuttle then passes below the first long strand and above the next. A device called a reed pushes the woven yarn together to tighten it.

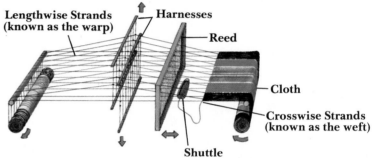

Lengthwise Strands (known as the warp)
Harnesses
Reed
Cloth
Crosswise Strands (known as the weft)
Shuttle

Weaver at Work *Denise Winders operates back-to-back looms. Shuttles contain the different colors of yarn used to help produce these plaid patterns.*

FREEZE-DRIED FOOD

You're going on a week-long camping trip deep into the woods. You'll need to take along enough food to last the whole trip. But how will you keep it fresh? Some food spoils if it is not kept cold. Canned food would be too heavy to carry. Freeze-dried food is the answer for this trip. It is lightweight—as much as 90 percent lighter than fresh food. And it lasts for years without being refrigerated.

To use freeze-dried food, you just add water. The food soaks up the water like a sponge. In just a few minutes, the dried food returns to its original shape and color.

A company in Albany, Oregon, makes many kinds of freeze-dried foods—from beans to beef stew. Oregon Freeze Dry Foods, Inc., makes such dishes by first cooking and freezing the food. Next, the water is removed. Then the food is put into an airtight package. After that, the dish is ready for a hungry camper like you to prepare and enjoy.

LIANE ENKELIS (ALL)

Outdoor Feast

Holli Jager, 9, and Jimmy Gilliam, 11, eat a meal of freeze-dried food near Holli's home, in Albany, Oregon. Holli's parents, Sandra and Norman Jager, prepared the four-dish meal.

Presto—Let's Eat!

Freeze-dried peaches (top, left) and a shrimp and rice dish (top, right) are dry before cooking. After boiling water has been added, the dishes are ready to eat in five to ten minutes (bottom).

Cooking Stage

Steam rises from a kettle in which food for a freeze-dried dish is cooking (below). A worker checks the temperature inside the kettle.

Freezing Food

Cooked food placed on trays is wheeled into a freezing tunnel. There, the food quickly freezes at a temperature of –20°F (–29°C). This worker wears a coat, gloves, and boots to protect him from the cold. The rack of food is attached to an overhead track. The track makes it easier to move the food into the freezing tunnel.

Removing Water

A worker notes the temperature inside a drying chamber (below). Frozen food is placed in this chamber. The air is pumped from the chamber, creating a vacuum. The food is then heated to about 100°F (38°C). Together, the heat and the vacuum remove 98 percent of the water from the food. The freeze-dried food is then ready for packaging.

Tasty Shrimp

Shrimp purchased already cooked and frozen is spread on trays. Workers will take the shrimp straight to the drying chamber.

Tiny 'Brain' *The gray square in the center of this picture, called an integrated circuit, regulates a quartz watch. The gold-colored metal strips around it carry electrical signals to other parts of the watch.*

WATCHES

A quartz watch gets its name from the tiny quartz crystal inside. A battery makes the crystal vibrate rapidly. Each time the crystal vibrates, it sends out a small electrical pulse.

The part of the watch called the integrated circuit counts these pulses and groups them into seconds, minutes, hours—and in some watches into days, months, and years! Here is how Texas Instruments Incorporated makes quartz watches in its Lubbock, Texas, factory.

Power Supply

A worker attaches a watch's battery connection. One battery will keep the watch running for about a year. Quartz watches often gain or lose as little as a minute a month.

IRA BLOCK (ALL)

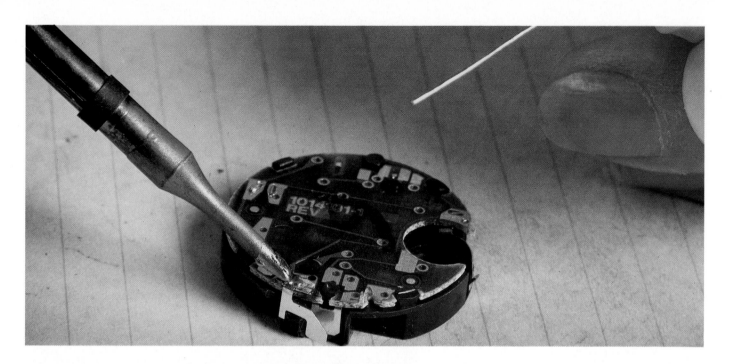

Adding a Spring

The flat gold spring above will be connected to a button used to set the watch. The hole on the right is where the battery will go.

Assembly Time

Workers in the background assemble watches (left). Those in the foreground put completed watches into boxes for shipping.

Watch Without Hands

The finished watch (below) shows the time in numerals. The buttons on the watch control such features as a calendar and a stopwatch.

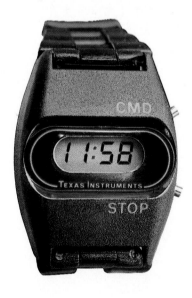

GRANDFATHER CLOCKS

It's hard to lose track of the time if you have a grandfather clock in your home. Most of these tall clocks chime every hour. Some even strike on the half hour and on the quarter hour.

Grandfather clocks have weights hanging from chains or ropes inside their cases. The pull of the weights keeps the clocks running. The clocks also have pendulums that swing back and forth to keep the clocks running at the correct speed. (See the diagram and the explanation of how a clock works on page 56.)

In International Falls, Minnesota, ninth-grade students can take a class called Clock Works. Each year, more than a hundred students make grandfather clock cases in this class. They start by learning to use woodworking tools safely. Then they cut out wood for the clock cases, put the cases together, and install the works. By the end of the year, each student has a completed grandfather clock.

54

Working Together

Students in International Falls, Minnesota, cut out pieces for grandfather clock cases (below). Class members cut out and assemble the frames of the clock cases as a group. Each student then gets a case to complete. Students learn techniques of the assembly line plus methods of individual craftsmanship.

REGENE RADNIECKI (ALL)

Personal Touch

David Hay, 15, adds an eagle to the top of his clock case (above). Students in the Clock Works class pay for all materials used in building their cases. They also pay for the clockwork, called a movement, that goes inside each case. These supplies cost about $250.

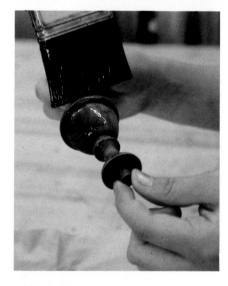

Finishing the Wood

With help from a friend, a student brushes a coat of lacquer on a clock ornament. Students sand their clock cases smooth, stain them to add color, then apply five coats of lacquer.

55

Oiling the Works *Heidi Baron, 15, oils a clock movement before it is put inside the case. The movement cost about $180.*

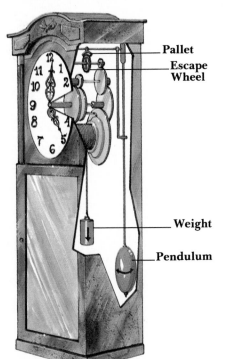

Pallet
Escape
Wheel

Weight

Pendulum

Inside Story

The drawing at left shows what makes a grandfather clock run. A weight inside the clock case powers the clock by pulling downward against a series of connected wheels. One of these, called the escape wheel, is connected to the pendulum by a device known as a pallet. Each time the pendulum swings, the pallet allows the escape wheel to move forward one notch. This moves the hands of the clock at the correct speed. The movement of the escape wheel against the pallet produces the clock's familiar ticking sound. Most grandfather clocks have to be wound once a week. Winding a clock lifts the weight back to its starting position.

Adding the Chimes

Clock Works teacher Wallace Haglund helps Brent Baron, 16, put the chimes into his case. Brent has already installed the clock face and the movement in his case.

Time To Be Proud

After working for a hundred hours during the school year, the students have finished their clocks. Most students will keep them. A few will sell their clocks for about $700.

REGENE RADNIECKI (ALL)

57

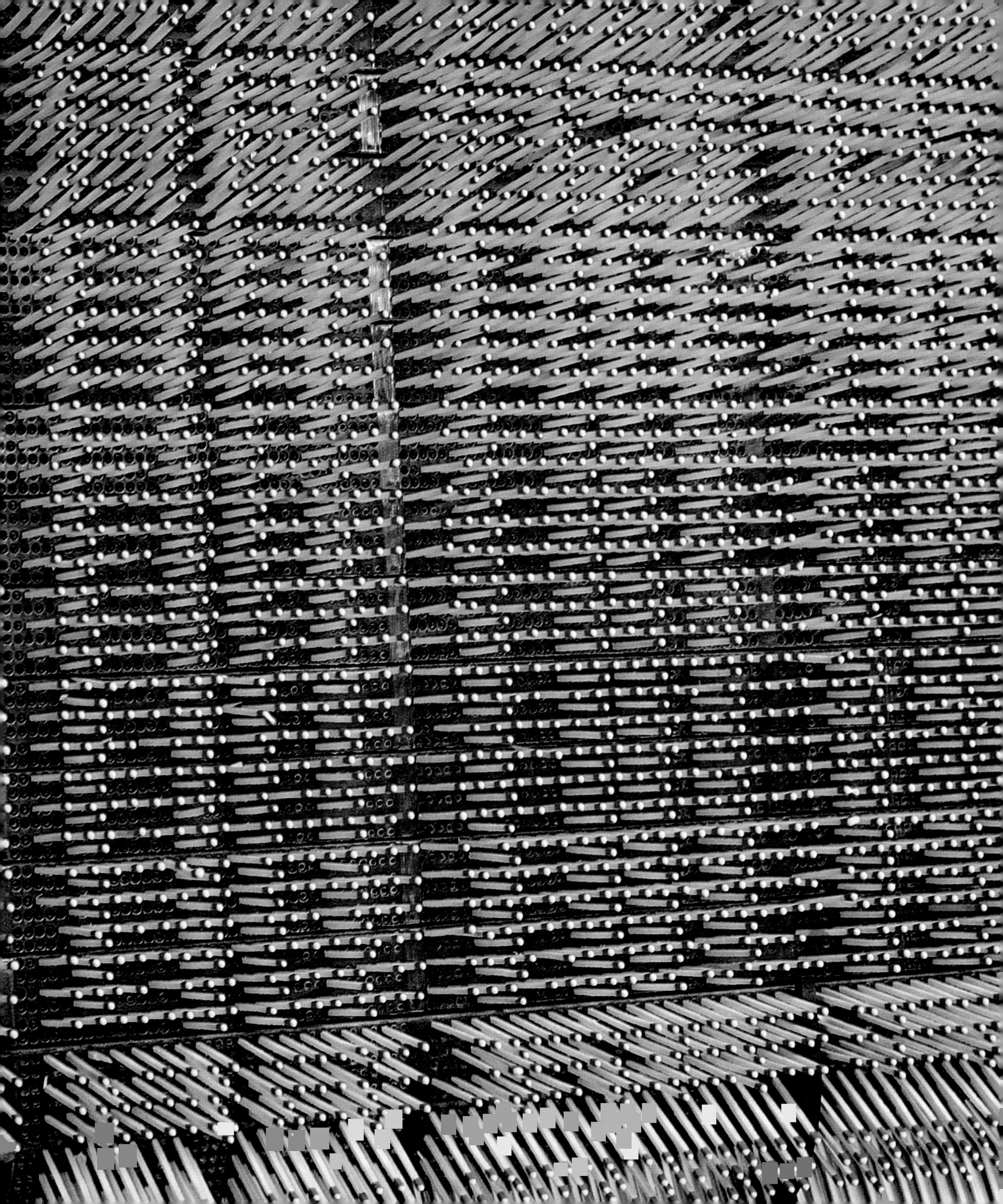

3

HOW LITTLE THINGS ARE MADE

Small objects often can be extremely important. Think of what would happen if you tried to ride your bicycle without the screws, nuts, and bolts that hold it together. You wouldn't get very far. Or what if you tried to put on a shirt and the buttons disappeared? You wouldn't be very well dressed.

A small object such as a hearing aid can produce big results. To the person wearing it, this device can mean the difference between hearing and not hearing.

Some 350 years ago, an English poet wrote about the importance of small things. He said: "For want of a nail the shoe is lost; for want of a shoe the horse is lost; for want of a horse the rider is lost." This poet, George Herbert, knew that even something as small as the nail that holds on a horseshoe can make a big difference.

Some items made today seem to keep getting smaller. For example, during the 1970s scientists invented a tiny object called a microprocessor. This small electronic device is the "brain" inside calculators, home video games, and other products.

Microprocessors replaced much larger devices that served the same function. Because of the reduced size of microprocessors, today's calculators are much smaller than earlier models. In fact, some wristwatches now contain tiny calculators.

On the pages that follow, you will see how a variety of little things are made. You will watch small sticks of wood being made into matches. You will see scraps of glass being turned into marbles. And you will learn how contact lenses are made from small pieces of plastic.

All in a Row

Tiny holes in a conveyor hold hundreds of wooden matchsticks. The holes keep the matchsticks in position while the heads of the matches are formed. Turn the page to see how matches are made.

IRA BLOCK

MATCHES

A wooden match looks as if it should be a simple thing to make. But it took inventors many years to develop a match that was safe to use and easy to manufacture. Until the mid-1800s, people made matches by hand. Not long after that, machines for making matches were developed. These machines allowed factories to produce millions of matches a day.

Wooden matchsticks usually are cut from aspen logs. The tips of the matchsticks are dipped in chemicals to form the heads. "Strike-anywhere" matches burst into flame when struck on any rough surface. "Safety" matches ignite only when struck against a special material on the outside of the matchbox or cover.

The Diamond Match factory, in Cloquet, Minnesota, can produce ten million matches an hour. The pictures here and on page 62 show how matches are made.

IRA BLOCK (BOTH)

Close Shave

Sharp blades trim bark from a log that will be cut into matchsticks. The blades are on a cylinder below the log. The two wheels above the log keep it turning so it will be trimmed evenly.

Mountain of Sticks

With a pitchfork, Marvin Pauna scoops up matchsticks in a storage room. He moves the sticks toward a conveyor system. From this storage area, the sticks will travel to machines that will add the match heads.

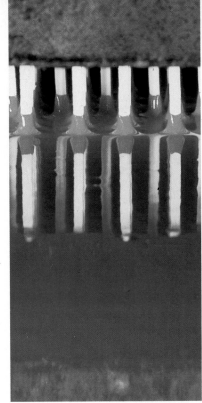

On With Their Heads!

Inside a match machine, sticks travel over a tray (above, left). The tray contains chemicals that will make the matches burn. The sticks are reflected in the chemicals. The tray is raised when the sticks are above it, and the ends of the sticks are dipped into the chemicals (above, center). The tray is then lowered. Small peaks form in the thick liquid below the dipped matchsticks (right). After these sticks have been dipped, another batch of sticks will roll into place. About 3,600 matchsticks are dipped at a time. The process takes only a few seconds.

Striking Tips

Heads are dipped into chemicals that form tips to ignite strike-anywhere matches (left). The matches later will pass through a drying chamber, then drop into a boxing machine.

Perfect Match

Finished matches fill cardboard boxes (below). The boxes will be inserted into covers.

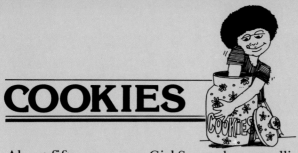

COOKIES

About fifty years ago, Girl Scouts began selling cookies to earn money for troop activities. At first, the girls sold cookies baked in their homes or by small local bakeries. Then in 1934, a large commercial bakery in Philadelphia, Pennsylvania, began making cookies especially for the Girl Scouts.

Today, Girl Scouts throughout the United States sell more than a hundred million boxes of cookies every year. Several companies bake these cookies. One is Little Brownie Bakers, of Louisville, Kentucky. This company makes seven kinds of Girl Scout cookies. The photograph below and those on the next two pages show how Little Brownie Bakers makes the cookies called Samoas.

IRA BLOCK

Dough for 45,000 Cookies *James Wright shovels a batch of cookie dough into a trough at Little Brownie Bakers. The dough is made of flour, shortening, and other ingredients. This batch weighs 1,500 pounds (680 kg).*

Ready to Bake

A roller with designs cut into it presses the dough into cookie shapes. A conveyor belt then carries the cookies to the oven.

Caramel Coating

Freshly baked cookies pass under a shower of hot caramel. A roller below the moving wire belt spreads more of the hot caramel on the bottoms of the cookies.

IRA BLOCK (ALL)

Coconut Bath

Sweetened, toasted coconut covers the cookies and sticks to the caramel (left). Blowers will remove the excess coconut, which will be used on other cookies.

Chocolate Stripes

Coconut-sprinkled Samoas pass under thin streams of melted chocolate (above). A roller underneath the wire belt coats the bottoms of the cookies with more chocolate.

On to the Cooler

Caramel-coated cookies move toward a cooling tunnel. There the syrupy coating will thicken. Coconut and chocolate will be added next.

Packed for Delivery

As finished cookies roll out of a final cooling tunnel, workers pack them in special trays (left). The trays keep the cookies from sticking together. Above, Girl Scouts Robyn Evers, left, and Akiko Herron, both 10, sell Samoas to Mrs. Cheryl Merrill, of Great Falls, Virginia.

65

MARBLES

People have been playing with marbles for hundreds of years. The first marbles were fruit pits, nuts, and round pebbles. In the 1700s, people began making small, hard balls from the stone called marble. That's where the name "marble" comes from.

Today, marbles manufactured in the United States are usually made of glass. Most of these are produced in four factories in West Virginia. Factories such as Marble King, Inc., in Paden City, West Virginia, produce millions of marbles each year. Marble King can make as many as 220 marbles a minute.

Marble factories make some of their products by melting scrap glass and reshaping it. They also make their own glass using a material called silica sand, plus other ingredients. Marble companies make many different types of marbles. These often have colorful names, such as glassies, cat's-eyes, and rainbows.

Some people play marbles for prizes. The National Marbles Tournament, held each year in Wildwood, New Jersey, awards $500 scholarships to the top two players. To learn the rules of the game played at this tournament, turn to page 9 of FAR-OUT FUN!

N.G.S. PHOTOGRAPHER JOSEPH H. BAILEY (ALL)

Recycling Glass

Scraps of glass such as these broken pieces are often used in making marbles.

Crunnnch!

A marble factory worker shovels pieces of broken glass into a machine that crushes them into bits. The crushed glass later will be melted down and shaped into marbles.

66

Round They Go

Red-hot glass that has been cut into small cubes drops into the shaping machine. The moving rollers of this machine give the marbles their round shape.

Colorful Assortment

Shiny new marbles roll toward the packaging machine. Stripes were added to the marbles by pouring melted colored glass into melted plain glass.

Bagful of Fun

A worker staples a label onto a bag of marbles. If she finds a faulty marble, she will replace it with one from the box in front of her. The bag is then ready for shipping.

Shooting To Win

Young marble shooters play a game called "ringer." The player who shoots the most marbles out of the ring wins. Playing are, from the left, Tanya Young, 12, Marcus Wigglesworth, 11, and Dene Lee, 12, all of Alexandria, Virginia.

JEWELRY

Mary Ehlers has a drawer that is filled with gold! Mary makes gold jewelry in her shop in Alexandria, Virginia. Each day, she works with gold, wax, plaster, and an assortment of unusual tools. She shapes objects in gold using an ancient technique called lost-wax casting.

To make an object, such as a ring, Mary first makes a wax model of her design. She uses dental tools and the heated point of an electric pen to shape the wax. Then she forms a plaster mold around the wax model.

Next, Mary puts the mold into a special oven called a kiln. Inside the kiln, the wax model melts away—or is "lost." This leaves a hole in the plaster shaped exactly like the ring. Mary then forces melted gold into the mold. When she puts the mold in water, the plaster breaks apart. What is left is a solid-gold version of her wax design!

N.G.S. PHOTOGRAPHER JOSEPH H. BAILEY (ALL)

Taking Shape

Mary Ehlers forms a model of a ring (below). She wraps wax rods around a tool called a mandrel. The mandrel helps her make the ring the right size. Mary will later cut off excess wax.

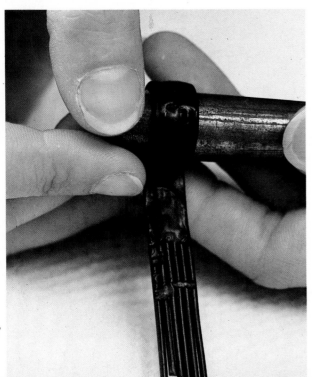

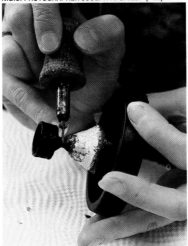

Adding Rods

Using an electric pen, Mary attaches wax rods to the ring model (above). The rods, when melted, will leave pathways for liquid gold to flow into the mold. Mary anchors the rods to a metal base (left). The base fits on the bottom of a special container. Mary will later pour plaster into the container.

Pouring the Mold

Mary fills the container with plaster, covering the wax ring model (right). In an hour, the plaster will harden. Mary then will heat the container. The wax will melt, leaving a hole in the shape of the ring.

Holder for Gold

A torch flame heats a container called a crucible. Gold will be melted inside this container. The crucible sits in a device called a centrifugal caster. After the mold is placed next to the crucible, the gold is melted and the casting arm is spun. This causes the melted gold to flow from the crucible into the mold.

Plaster
Wax Ring Model
Mold After Wax Has Melted

Crucible

Mold

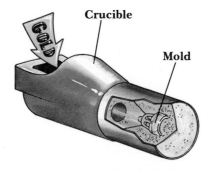

Gold Ring

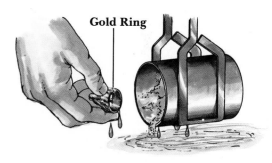

Lost-wax Casting

Plaster hardens around the wax ring model (above, left). When the plaster is heated, the wax melts and drains out. The plaster is then heated further to burn away all traces of wax. This leaves a hollow mold.

Gold is melted in the crucible after the mold is in place. The crucible and the mold are spun, forcing the gold into the mold. There, the gold hardens into the shape of a ring.

The plaster mold, with gold inside, is lowered into water. The plaster breaks apart, freeing the ring. Excess gold is trimmed from the ring.

Shining Example

A rapidly whirling tool smooths the newly molded ring. Mary polishes each new ring for more than an hour to remove tiny scratches. Unpolished gold looks dull.

CONTACT LENSES

You wouldn't normally stick something into your eye on purpose. But millions of people do just that every day. The objects these people put into their eyes are contact lenses.

Contacts are plastic disks not much bigger than shirt buttons. The lenses are made in pairs, one lens for each eye. To put in contacts, you place one lens at a time on a fingertip. Then you gently touch it to your eyeball. The lens clings to the film of moisture on your cornea. The cornea is the thin tissue covering the colored part of your eye.

Contact lenses, like glasses, are designed to correct vision problems. To fit comfortably, each lens must be shaped to the size and the curve of the wearer's eyeball. Contacts come in hard and soft models. Hard lenses are made of firm plastic. Soft contacts are made of plastic that is kept flexible by moisture.

The soft contacts shown on these pages start out as small pieces of hard plastic. A special process later softens the plastic. Many people think soft lenses are more comfortable than hard ones. Some people prefer contact lenses to regular glasses because contacts don't change the appearance of the face.

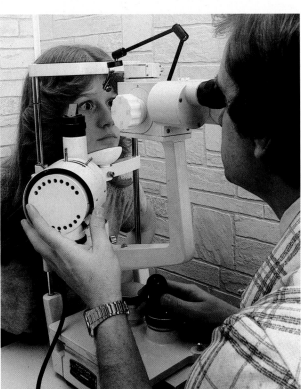

N.G.S. PHOTOGRAPHER BIANCA LAVIES (ALL)

How Do They Feel?

Dr. Jay Rubin checks the fit of 13-year-old Jennifer Jordan's new soft contact lenses. He uses an instrument called a biomicroscope. Jennifer lives in Oxon Hill, Maryland.

Molds for Contacts

Drops of liquid plastic fill small molds. The plastic will harden in about six hours to form "buttons." These will be shaped into contacts.

Open Wide!

Jennifer carefully puts a new contact in her eye. "It isn't very comfortable to open your eyes so wide," she says. "But you get used to it." When Jennifer isn't wearing her contacts, she leaves them in a special solution. This keeps them from drying out and becoming hard. Not all vision problems can be corrected with contact lenses.

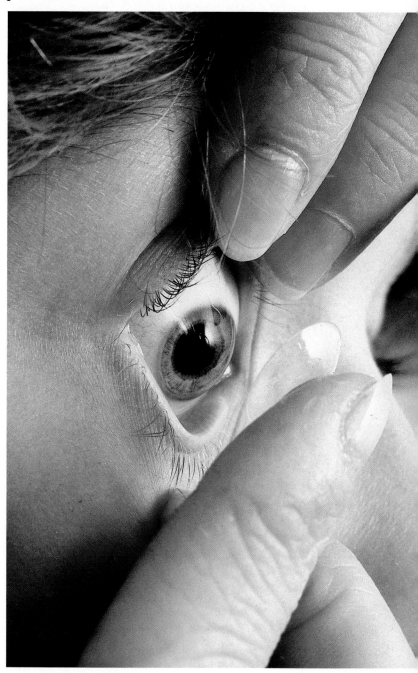

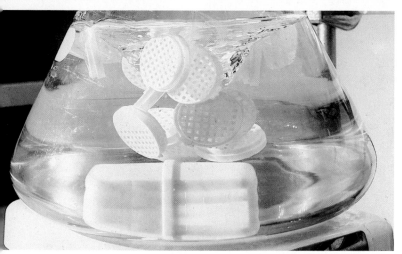

Shaping and Softening

Newly made buttons tumble from their molds (top, left). After they are carefully inspected for flaws, the buttons are cut to the correct prescriptions. A diamond-tipped tool cuts the proper curves in a button (top, right). Both sides of the button are shaped with this tool. After being shaped, a lens is only about one-tenth of a millimeter thick. Lenses then soak in a mixture of boiling water and salt for several hours (above). The plastic absorbs the water and becomes soft.

STICK-ON BANDAGES

Bandages help injuries heal faster by keeping out germs that cause infections. Long ago, bandages were simply strips of cloth. Then in the late 1800s, people started soaking the strips in substances that made them both sticky and waterproof. About 1900, people began bandaging injuries with gauze pads held in place by sticky cloth tape.

Today, most adhesive bandages are made of waterproof plastic. The bandages have gauze pads in the center, and they usually have holes in them that allow air to reach the injury. Modern bandages stick tightly, yet can be peeled off easily. Here you can see how the Kendall Company, of Franklin, Kentucky, makes bandages that have baseball emblems printed on them.

BILL STRODE (BOTH)

Sticky Start

A long plastic sheet coated with adhesive (above) passes through an oven. The overhead lights dry the adhesive. Baseball emblems have already been printed on the other side of the sheet.

From One to Many

Rolled on a drum, the coated plastic (right) goes through a slitting machine. The machine cuts the plastic into narrower rolls. Turn the page to see how the rolls are made into bandages.

Soft Centers *As a small roll of plastic passes through a finishing machine, a mechanical arm stamps on soft gauze pads. The plastic will be cut into bandages. Each one will be wrapped, then packaged.*

Germfree Finish

Stacked in boxes, bandages are put into a chamber called a sterilizer (above). Inside the chamber, gas, heat, and steam kill germs. The sterilizer holds about 500,000 bandages at once. After tests show that they are free of germs, the bandages are ready for use (right).

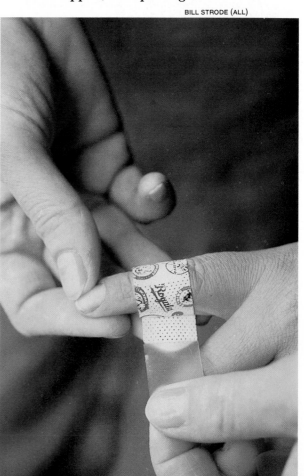

74

TINY FURNITURE

Bill Robertson likes to think small. Robertson, of Wheaton, Maryland, builds miniature furniture such as the 3-inch-tall (8-cm) desk below. He builds the furniture for collectors.

As many as 200,000 people in the United States collect tiny creations like those Robertson makes. These people collect everything from miniature desks to tiny television sets. Robertson began making miniatures $3\frac{1}{2}$ years ago. In addition to desks, he builds clocks, tables, and other items.

Robertson copies his miniatures from full-size pieces. To see how he builds a tiny grandfather clock that actually works, turn the page.

JOHN MCDONNELL

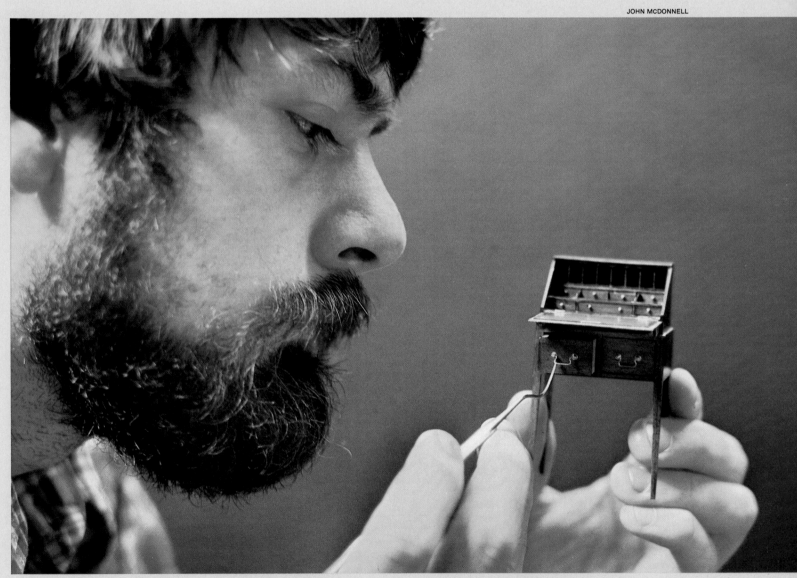

Attention to Detail *Bill Robertson adjusts a drawer in a miniature desk that he built. The drawers open and close just like those in a full-size desk.*

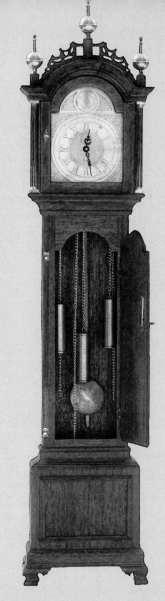

Craftsman at Work

Robertson assembles a miniature grandfather clock in his workshop (left). He puts the clock together with glue and tiny screws. Robertson first obtained detailed drawings of a full-size clock. He used the drawings as a guide in cutting and shaping the wood and the metal parts of the miniature. The small clock contains about 75 pieces of wood and 120 pieces of metal. Some of the parts and tools Robertson uses lie on a sheet of stamps below.

Completed Timepiece

The 8-inch-tall (20-cm) clock at right is one-twelfth the size of the original clock. The miniature, which runs on the works from a small watch, will sell for about $1,800.

Small World

With a magnifying glass held to his eye, Robertson uses a small file to smooth a miniature key. Each of these keys is about a quarter of an inch (6 mm) long. Robertson makes the keys for his tiny clocks and desks.

4

HOW BIG THINGS ARE MADE

Building Giants

Workers finish putting together a Boeing 747 jumbo jet. This jet is being assembled inside one of the world's largest buildings, in Everett, Washington. Turn the page to see how 747s are built.

THE BOEING COMPANY

Big things are all around us. Huge trucks travel on highways that are six lanes wide. People live and work in towering buildings. Some of the steel and concrete skyscrapers in our cities rise more than 1,000 feet (300 m) into the air.

When we go on vacation, we may cross the country in a large jet. Or we may travel across the ocean in a ship that is hundreds of feet long. If we travel by car, we may drive across a bridge that stretches more than a mile and a half (2,400 m) in length.

Most of the world's large structures have been built in the last few hundred years. But people of long ago built big things, too. Think of the buildings of ancient Greece, the pyramids of Egypt, and the Maya temples of Mexico and Central America.

Building big things has always been a big job. Scientists believe that to raise the pyramids of Egypt, workers constructed long ramps made of mud bricks. Then they dragged the heavy stones needed for the pyramids up the ramps.

Many ancient structures took years to build—sometimes even centuries. Today, a tall building often can be finished in little more than a year. Huge pieces of construction equipment help make this possible. For example, you may have seen giant cranes lifting steel beams into the air at building sites.

On the following pages, you will watch people putting together several big things. You will see how a company produces fireworks that light up the sky. You will watch workers constructing a long bridge. And you will learn how a large ride is built for an amusement park.

JUMBO JETS

Orville and Wilbur Wright made the world's first successful powered airplane flight in 1903. Their small propeller plane traveled about 120 feet (37 m) in the air. That same flight today could take place on the wings of a 747 jet airliner—with room to spare.

The Wright brothers would be amazed if they could see one of these jets. The wings of a 747 stretch more than 195 feet (59 m) from tip to tip. The plane's tail is as tall as a five-story building, and its wings have more surface area than a basketball court does.

Engineers at the Boeing Company, in Seattle, Washington, designed the 747 jumbo jet in the 1960s. Containing 4½ million parts, the 747 is the world's largest jet airliner.

Pilots say the 747 handles easily, even though it is large. Many of its controls are computerized. Passengers like the plane's roomy cabin. International travelers appreciate its nonstop flights—some 747s can fly nearly 7,000 miles (11,000 km) without stopping to refuel. That's as far as flying from New York City to London, England, and back again.

The Wright brothers built their plane inside a building. Planes are still made that way. In Everett, Washington, the Boeing Company constructed a huge building in which to assemble the 747. The ten-story-high structure is big enough to cover 47 football fields.

Final assembly of each 747 takes about one month, with work going on around the clock. By the time a plane rolls onto the runway, about 10,000 people have worked on it.

Keeping Track of Parts

A worker labels aluminum tubes (right). The tubes will carry a special fluid throughout the aircraft. The fluid is part of the plane's hydraulic system. This system operates many moving parts, such as the landing gear. A 747 contains about 2,000 pieces of tubing.

Miles of Wires

Specialists arrange bundles of electrical wires (above) that will go into a 747. Each jet contains more than 100 miles (161 km) of wiring.

Get Up and Go

Four huge engines (above) power each jumbo jet. The engines drive the 747s forward at speeds of more than 600 miles (966 km) an hour.

Wing Workers

Technicians assemble a 747 wing (above). The man on top fastens on part of the surface of the wing. The man below works on the inside of the wing where it will be joined to the frame of the plane.

Taking Shape

A crane lowers the rear section of a 747 body into place. The wings have been joined to the center section, and the front section has been lowered into place.

THE BOEING COMPANY (ALL)

Ready to Fly

The drawing at right shows a completed 747. This jumbo jet can carry 452 people in its cabin. A newer version of the plane can carry 550 passengers. Workers at the Boeing Company plant in Everett, Washington, can build a dozen 747s at a time. Crews complete an average of seven planes a month. Nearly five hundred 747s are now in service around the world.

Big Paint Job

Standing on a platform, a worker sprays paint on the assembled tail of a jumbo jet. Many airlines buy 747s from the Boeing Company. Each airline has its own colors and markings.

Inside Installation

A technician installs air, light, and oxygen equipment in an overhead cabin compartment.

Ground Testing

Engineers test the controls of a 747 before it is taken up for its first flight. The man on the left wears a headset. With this, he can talk to people outside the plane to see if it is responding to the controls properly.

83

PAPER

Did you know that the paper this book is printed on was once part of a tree? Most paper is made from a material called cellulose. Trees and other plants contain this material. The cellulose fibers in trees are held together by a kind of natural glue called lignin.

To make paper such as the type used in this book, wood is first cut into chips. The lignin is then removed from the cellulose fibers. The fibers are mixed with water to form a pulp.

Pumps spray the pulp onto a large moving screen in the papermaking machine. Most of the water in the pulp drains through the screen, leaving an even mat of fibers.

This mat passes through a series of rollers that remove the rest of the water and press the fibers together. The result is paper!

Future Paper

A forester in Arkansas plants pine seedlings. He uses a tool called a dibble to make a hole in the ground. In 30 to 35 years, these trees will be cut down and made into paper and other products.

Trainload of Wood

Harvested pine trees (above) arrive at a papermaking plant in Crossett, Arkansas. The wood will be cut into chips and stored in huge piles like those shown here. The chips will later be moved to a nearby paper mill. Turn the page to see how the Georgia-Pacific Corporation produces tissue paper from chips of wood.

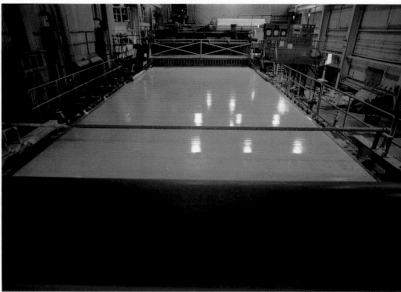

Making Pulp

Wood chips such as those on the previous page have been turned into pulp. The chips were cooked along with chemicals. The watery mixture here is called pulp slurry.

Starting Paper

Pulp slurry sprays onto a fast-moving wire screen. Water drains through the screen, leaving behind a layer of cellulose fibers. A series of rollers will squeeze out more water and press the fibers tightly together.

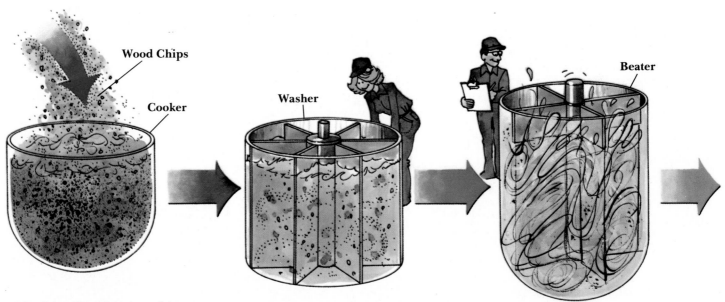

Wood Chips

Cooker

Washer

Beater

Machine for Papermaking

Wood chips cook in a chemical solution in the first part of the drawing above. The chemicals remove the wood's natural glue and break down the chips into a pulp. The pulp is then washed and bleached, beaten to the proper thickness, *and pumped onto a moving screen. Water from the pulp drains through holes in the screen. Rollers squeeze more water from the pulp. Heated rollers dry the wet paper. The finished paper forms a roll at the end of the machine.*

Finishing Paper

A worker checks to see that the paper is moving at the right speed through the finishing end of the machine. Here, the fibers are pressed into a solid sheet. Heated rollers dry the sheet.

Checking Quality

Finished paper winds onto a roll at the end of the machine. An expert checks the paper by tapping it with a stick. He can tell its quality by listening to the sound produced. The large roll later will be cut into smaller sizes.

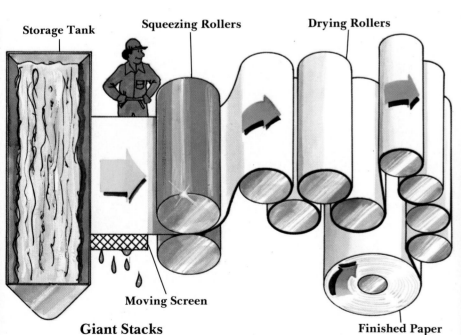

Storage Tank

Squeezing Rollers

Drying Rollers

Moving Screen

Finished Paper

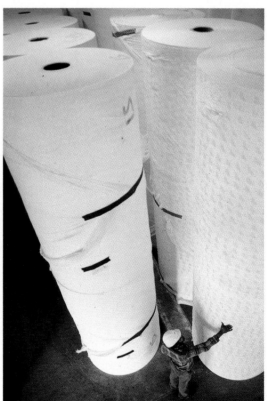

Giant Stacks

Rolls of tissue paper (right) are ready to be made into napkins, paper towels, and other products. A worker is dwarfed by the stacks of huge rolls.

FIREWORKS

The loud booms and the sparkling colors made by fireworks often add the finishing touch to celebrations. Historians believe the Chinese were the first to make fireworks.

About a thousand years ago, the Chinese put an explosive material called black powder inside hollow sections of bamboo. When lit, these early fireworks exploded loudly. In the 1800s, people learned how to mix certain chemicals with black powder to produce beautiful colors.

In the middle of the 1800s, members of the Grucci family began making fireworks in Italy. Today, this family runs the New York Pyrotechnic Products Company, in Bellport, New York. "Pyrotechnics" (say pie-ruh-TEK-nix) is another word for fireworks.

The Grucci family makes fireworks for large displays such as the one at the 1980 Winter Olympics (left). Here and on the following pages, you can see how the Gruccis make fireworks for such exhibitions.

CLAYTON J. PRICE (BOTH)

Warning Sign

A sign at the Grucci fireworks factory, in Bellport, New York (above), cautions people that fireworks can be dangerous.

Beautiful Display

Brilliant fireworks (left) surround the symbol of the 1980 Winter Olympics, in Lake Placid, New York. The Gruccis made these fireworks.

KEN CLARK

Safety First

Steve Valenti uses a face mask and a cap to keep powders that go into fireworks from getting into his nose, throat, and hair. Valenti holds a sifter that is used to remove lumps from the powders before they are mixed together.

Color and Noise

The ingredients at right drive fireworks into the sky and produce beautiful colors and loud booms. Black powder causes a firework to shoot upward. Bright colors are produced by charcoal and by the chemicals called barium chlorate, red gum, dextrin, and potassium perchlorate. Potassium perchlorate also causes loud explosions.

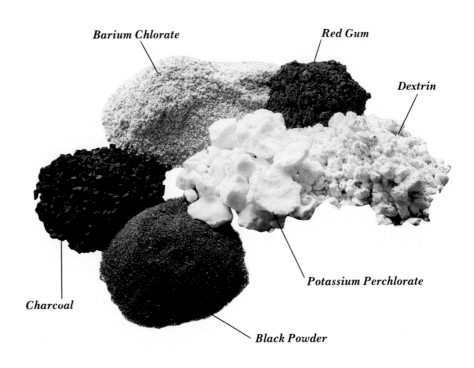

Barium Chlorate

Red Gum

Dextrin

Charcoal

Potassium Perchlorate

Black Powder

Sifting Powder

A worker sifts a chemical to remove the lumps (above, left). Lumps must be removed before chemicals can be mixed. Another worker (above, center) pours chemicals into cardboard tubes. These will be put inside fireworks.

Ready for Assembly

The way a firework bursts in the sky depends on how all the above parts are put together. The diagram on page 91 shows how the finished product works.

Adding Fuses

Taping on delay fuses, Cindy Crespi finishes the noisemaking part of fireworks (left). The delay fuse makes this section, called the salute, explode after the firework is in the air. One or more salutes go into a larger tube, along with the chemicals that produce the colors. The black powder that drives the firework into the air is put in the bottom of the tube. A long fuse is added to ignite the powder, and the tube is wrapped in paper.

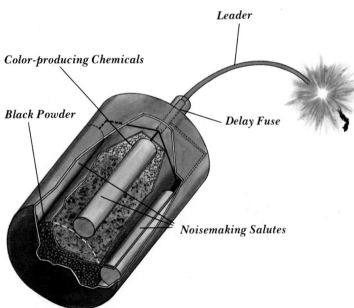

Leader

Color-producing Chemicals

Black Powder

Delay Fuse

Noisemaking Salutes

How a Firework Works

To set off the completed firework (above), you light the long fuse, or leader. The leader sets off the black powder at the bottom of the tube. The powder burns quickly, lifting the firework several hundred feet into the air. The leader also sets off the delay fuse attached to the salutes. After the firework is in the air, the delay fuse ignites the salutes and the color-producing chemicals. The result—loud explosions and bright colors.

This drawing of the Dumbarton Bridge over San Francisco Bay, in California, shows

BRIDGES

A stream blocks your way during a hike in the woods. You can't jump across because the stream is too wide. Then you see a long tree branch lying nearby. That gives you an idea.

You put the branch over the stream. Now, balancing carefully, you cross over the water. You are a bridge builder! Your bridge didn't take long to make. But think how many years and how much money it takes to build a bridge over a bay or a wide river.

The Dumbarton Bridge over San Francisco Bay, in California, is shown here and on the following pages. It has taken nearly four years to build. When completed in mid-1981, it will have cost about fifty million dollars.

This huge structure is 8,600 feet (2,621 m) long and 85 feet (26 m) high in the middle. The new bridge will replace an old one that is now too small for today's amount of traffic.

From the Bottom Up

To build a bridge over deep water, workers first put groups of concrete supports, called piles, into the water. A heavy hammer drives the piles deep into the earth under the water. The tops of the piles stick out just above the water level. Workers next build vertical and horizontal supports on top of the piles. The vertical supports, called piers, are like the legs of a table. The horizontal supports, called girders, link the bridge's piers. The roadway of the bridge is then built on top of the girders.

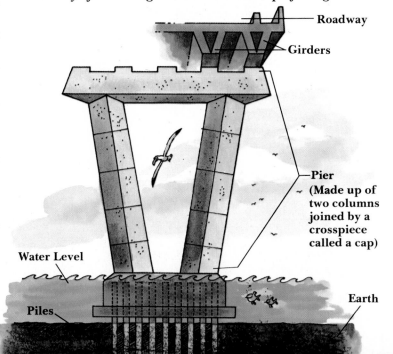

Roadway

Girders

Pier
(Made up of two columns joined by a crosspiece called a cap)

Water Level

Piles

Earth

how the bridge will look when it is completed in mid-1981.

Building Above Water

A crane lowers a concrete panel into place (below). Panels are joined to form walls around the top of each group of piles. Concrete is then poured inside the walls to form a support for the pier. The old Dumbarton Bridge is at left.

Reaching Skyward

A worker adds steel bars to one column of a pier that is being built (below). Later, temporary sides will be placed around the steel bars. Concrete will then be poured inside. The steel will add strength to the concrete.

Rows of Piers

Completed piers stand like mighty legs. Concrete caps on top of the piers support girders. The bridge's roadway will be built on top of the girders.

Long Haul

A series of conveyors carries concrete from the truck in the background to an unfinished section of roadway. This section cannot yet safely support the weight of the truck. The truck must be unloaded on a part of the roadway that has been completed.

LIANE ENKELIS (ALL)

End of the Line

Concrete pours from the last conveyor. The worker moves the conveyor from side to side to cover all the roadway.

Smooth Touch

A wide finishing machine (above) levels and smooths concrete. One worker spreads concrete in front of the machine. Another worker, right, smooths concrete the machine cannot reach.

Bird's-eye View

The roadway appears in several stages at right. In the front, girders lie on top of piers. In the middle, girders have been joined by steel plates. In the back, the roadway has been completed.

Thrill Rides *Side-by-side flume rides snake their way around Marriott's Great America in Santa Clara, California. The rides are*

FLUMES

Imagine shooting down a narrow stream in a log boat at nearly 40 miles (64 km) an hour. The stream twists and turns, rises and falls—almost like a roller coaster.

This stream is called a flume ride. Flume rides are found at many amusement parks around the country. Instead of having cars that run on tracks, a flume ride has small boats that float inside a long trough filled with water.

The trough is made of concrete or of a strong material called fiberglass. It is mounted on steel or wooden supports. Pumps keep water flowing through the trough. Electric motors power a conveyor belt that lifts the boats to the top of the trough to start the ride.

Arrow Development Company, of Mountain View, California, built the flume rides at left. The picture below and those on the next two pages show how such rides are made.

Building a Trough

A worker sprays a substance called resin on the underside of a flume trough. The sticky resin holds strips of fiberglass cloth in place. The fiberglass helps make the trough stronger.

LIANE ENKELIS (BOTH)

60 feet (18 m) high in places and nearly 2,000 feet (610 m) long. A trip around either ride lasts about four minutes.

97

Finished Trough

A driver moves a section of finished trough to a storage area. From there, the sections are taken to amusement parks, where they are bolted together. Some flume rides contain more than a hundred sections of trough.

Sparks Fly

Torches cut a steel brake for the underside of a boat. The brake will keep the boat from rolling backward while it is being lifted to the top of the ride.

LIANE ENKELIS (ALL)

Wheels for Boats

The wheels above will be added to boats. Each boat has eight wheels—four to guide it inside the trough and four to support it in down chutes and at the end of the ride. One worker adds a wheel to a boat (right), and another installs a seat.

Big Finish

A spray of water means that another trip around the flume ride is almost over. Deeper water near the end of the ride causes the splash. The deeper water also slows down the boat.

FACTORY TOURS

Seeing firsthand how an item is made can be fascinating. Listed below are 24 free factory tours that offer a variety of interesting sights. Of course, these are only a few of the hundreds of tours available. To find out about other tours, call or write to local chambers of commerce or to state travel offices. If you are interested in a particular factory, find out if it has a tour or if it will arrange one. Be sure to ask if there are age restrictions. Most tours are not given on holidays, and most require that anyone under 16 be accompanied by an adult. It is a good idea to call before you go to any factory you'd like to tour.

BANDERA HAT COMPANY, 320 South Lake, Fort Worth, Texas 76104. Telephone: (817) 332-1541. *Tour description:* See western hats being made. *Length:* 30 minutes. *Schedule:* Monday through Friday, from 8 a.m. to 4 p.m. Advance notice is required.

BUREAU OF ENGRAVING AND PRINTING, 14th and C Streets S.W., Washington, D. C. 20228. Telephone: (202) 447-0261. *Tour description:* See various operations in the making of United States paper money. *Length:* 25 minutes. *Schedule:* Monday through Friday, from 8 a.m. to 2 p.m., except holidays. *Restrictions:* No cameras.

C. F. MARTIN AND COMPANY, 510 Sycamore Street, Nazareth, Pennsylvania 18064. Telephone: (215) 759-2837. *Tour description:* Follow the process of guitar construction from the preparation of the wood to the finished guitar. *Length:* One hour. *Schedule:* Monday through Friday, at 10:30 a.m. and 1:15 p.m.

COLEMAN COMPANY, INC., 597 North 1500 West Street, Cedar City, Utah 84720. Telephone: (801) 586-9437. *Tour description:* Get an in-depth look at all the steps in making tents, sleeping bags, and backpacks. *Length:* 45 minutes. *Schedule:* Monday through Friday, from 8 a.m. to 2 p.m. One day's notice is required.

CRYSTAL CREAM AND BUTTER COMPANY, 1013 D Street, Sacramento, California 95806. Telephone: (916) 444-7200. *Tour description:* See the processing of milk and other dairy products, including filling and packaging operations. *Length:* 30 to 45 minutes. *Schedule:* October through May: Mondays, Tuesdays, and Thursdays, from 9:30 a.m. to 3:45 p.m. Two weeks' notice is required. *Restrictions:* Visitors must be at least 6 years old. Groups are limited to 15 people.

DEKLOMP WOODEN SHOE AND DELFT FACTORY, 257 East 32nd Street, Holland, Michigan 49423. Telephone: (616) 396-2292. *Tour description:* Watch craftsmen making authentic Dutch wooden shoes. See artists painting the traditional Dutch blue-and-white delft china. *Length:* 30 minutes. *Schedule:* Monday through Saturday, from 9 a.m. to 5:30 p.m. Open Sundays during May. Advance notice is appreciated.

FENTON ART GLASS COMPANY, Caroline Avenue, Williamstown, West Virginia 26187. Telephone: (304) 375-7772. *Tour description:* Watch master craftsmen make bowls, vases, lamps, and other glassware by hand. *Length:* 35 minutes. *Schedule:* June, July, August: Monday through Friday, from 8:40 a.m. to 7:20 p.m. September through May: Mondays, Wednesdays, and Fridays, from 8:40 a.m. to 4:20 p.m.; Tuesdays and Thursdays, from 8:40 a.m. to 7:20 p.m. No tours during the first two weeks of July. *Restrictions:* Visitors must be at least 2 years old.

HAMPSHIRE PEWTER COMPANY, New Hampshire Route 28, Wolfeboro Center, New Hampshire 03894. Telephone: (603) 569-4944. *Tour description:* See master craftsmen cast and finish pewter tankards, candlesticks, plates, and award plaques. *Length:* 20 minutes. *Schedule:* Monday through Friday, on the hour from 9 a.m. to 4 p.m.

HILLERICH & BRADSBY COMPANY, INC., 1525 Charlestown-New Albany Road, Jeffersonville, Indiana 47130. Telephone: (812) 288-6611. *Tour description:* See how the famous baseball bat, the "Louisville Slugger," is shaped, sanded, and branded with the company's seal and the signatures of today's baseball stars. *Length:* 45 minutes. *Schedule:* Monday through Friday, at 10:30 a.m. and 2:30 p.m. Plant is closed on holidays, the last week of June, and the first two weeks of July. *Restrictions:* No cameras.

KODAK ELMGROVE PLANT, 901 Elmgrove Road, Rochester, New York 14650. Telephone: (716) 726-3426.
KODAK PARK, 200 Ridge Road West, Rochester, New York 14650. Telephone: (716) 722-2465. *Tour descriptions:* At Kodak Park, the company's largest manufacturing facility, take a behind-the-scenes look at how film and photographic paper are made. At the Elmgrove Plant, see cameras and projectors being made. *Length:* 1½ hours. *Schedule:* Monday through Friday, at 9:30 a.m. and 1:30 p.m. *Restrictions:* No cameras. Visitors must be at least 5 years old.

McMAHAN FURNITURE COMPANY, 615 West Main Street, Campbellsville, Kentucky 42718. Telephone: (502) 465-4831. *Tour description:* See all phases in the making of Early American furniture. Most of the work is done by hand. *Length:* 30 to 60 minutes. *Schedule:* Monday through Friday, from 8 a.m. to 3 p.m.

MILTON BRADLEY COMPANY, 443 Shaker Road (Route 220), East Longmeadow, Massachusetts 01028. Telephone: (413) 525-6411, extension 212. *Tour description:* Get a closeup look at all the steps in the manufacturing of games. *Length:* 1 to 1½ hours. *Schedule:* Wednesdays, from 9 a.m. to 2 p.m. Must make appointment four weeks in advance. *Restrictions:* No cameras. Visitors must be at least 8 years old.

O'BRIEN CORPORATION, 2700 Glynn Avenue (Highway 17 North), Brunswick, Georgia 31521. Telephone: (912) 265-7650. *Tour description:* See the complete process of paint manufacturing. *Length:* 45 minutes. *Schedule:* Monday through Thursday, from 10 to 11:30 a.m. and 2 to 3:30 p.m. One week's notice is required. *Restrictions:* Visitors must be at least 8 years old.

OLD WARKWORTH CHEESE FACTORY, 194 Hastings Road, Warkworth, Ontario, Canada, K0K 3K0. Telephone: (705) 924-2733. *Tour description:* See the making of old-style cheddar cheese. *Length:* No time limit. *Schedule:* May 24 through Thanksgiving, Saturdays only.

RAINBOW BAKING COMPANY, 111 Montano Road N.E., Albuquerque, New Mexico 87107. Telephone: (505) 345-3481. *Tour description:* Watch the complete process of baking bread and buns, beginning with sacks of flour and ending with packaged products. *Length:* One hour. *Schedule:* Mid-September to mid-May: Monday through Friday, from 9 a.m. to 3 p.m., by appointment. *Restrictions:* No cameras.

RAY HOLES SADDLE COMPANY, 213 West Main Street, Grangeville, Idaho 83530. Telephone: (208) 983-1460. *Tour description:* See what's involved in making custom western saddles and other riding equipment. *Length:* 30 minutes. *Schedule:* Monday through Friday, from 9 a.m. to 4 p.m. One day's notice is required for groups with more than four members.

ROYAL CANADIAN MINT, 520 Lagimodière Boulevard, Winnipeg, Manitoba, Canada, R2J 3E7. Telephone: (204) 257-3359. *Tour description:* Watch strips of metal being transformed into coins that are then inspected, counted, and bagged. *Length:* 40 minutes. *Schedule:* Every half hour Monday through Friday, from 9 a.m. to 3 p.m. One day's notice is required for large groups.

SUN PETROLEUM PRODUCTS COMPANY, 1700 South
Union, Tulsa, Oklahoma 74102. Telephone:
(918) 586-7301. *Tour description:* See the step-
by-step process that transforms crude oil into
lubrication oil and gasoline. *Length:* 1 to
1½ hours. *Schedule:* Monday through Friday, at
10 a.m. and 2 p.m.; Saturdays, at 10 a.m.
Restrictions: No flash photography.

SUPERIOR FIRE APPARATUS COMPANY, Joslyn and
Leslie Streets, Helena, Montana 59601.
Telephone: (406) 442-0745. *Tour description:*
Watch fire engines being built. *Length:*
One hour. *Schedule:* By appointment.
Restrictions: Visitors must be at least
6 years old.

TONKA TOYS, 5300 Shoreline Boulevard, Mound,
Minnesota 55364. Telephone: (612) 472-
8000. *Tour description:* See parts pressed out of
steel, painted, and assembled into toys.
Length: 45 minutes. *Schedule:* Tuesdays and
Fridays, at 9:30 and 10:45 a.m., and at 12:30
and 2 p.m. Reservations required. *Restrictions:*
Visitors must be at least 5 years old.
No cameras.

TURNCRAFT CLOCK IMPORTS COMPANY, 611
Winnetka Avenue North, Golden Valley,
Minnesota 55427. Telephone: (612) 544-1711.
Tour description: Tour the woodworking
shop and see how clock cases are made.
Length: One hour. *Schedule:* Monday through
Friday, from 10 a.m. to 5 p.m. Advance
notice is required.

U. S. MINT, 5th and Arch Streets, Philadelphia,
Pennsylvania 19106. Telephone: (215) 597-
2471. *Tour description:* From a glass-enclosed
gallery, see the entire coinage operation of
the world's largest mint. *Length:* 45 minutes.
Schedule: Monday through Friday, from
8:30 a.m. to 4 p.m.

WHEELER MANUFACTURING COMPANY, INC.,
107 Main Avenue, Lemmon, South Dakota
57638. Telephone: (605) 374-3848. *Tour
description:* Watch gemstones being cut and
polished, then made into rings, pendants,
and earrings. *Length:* One hour. *Schedule:*
Monday through Friday, from 8 a.m. to
4 p.m., by appointment.

INDEX

Bold type refers to illustrations; regular type refers to text.

Composition for HOW THINGS ARE MADE by National Geographic's Photographic Services, Carl M. Shrader, Chief; Lawrence F. Ludwig, Assistant Chief. Printed and bound by Holladay-Tyler Printing Corp., Rockville, Maryland. Color separations by The Lanman Companies, Washington, D. C.; Progressive Color Corp., Rockville, Maryland; Lincoln Graphics, Inc., Cherry Hill, New Jersey. Classroom Activities Folder produced by Mazer Corporation, Dayton, Ohio.

Library of Congress CIP Data
How things are made.
   (Books for world explorers)
   Bibliography: p.
   Includes index.
   SUMMARY: Explains how a variety of products—such as kaleidoscopes, baseballs, marbles, matches, toothpaste, light bulbs, and bridges—are made, highlighting the ways in which manufacturing techniques have changed over the years. A wall poster and a 24-page booklet of games and puzzles are included.
   1. Manufacturing processes—Juvenile literature. [1. Manufactures] I. National Geographic Society, Washington, D. C. II. Series.
TS183.H68   670   79-3242
ISBN 0-87044-334-8 (regular binding)
ISBN 0-87044-339-9 (library binding)

ADDITIONAL READING

Readers may want to check the National Geographic Index in a school or public library for related articles and to refer to the following books: Brown, A. E., and Jeffcott, H. A., *Absolutely Mad Inventions* (Dover Publications, Inc., 1960). Burns, Marilyn, *This Book Is About Time* (Little, Brown, and Company, 1978). Clarke, Donald, ed., *The Encyclopedia of How It's Built* (A & W, 1979); *The Encyclopedia of How It's Made* (A & W, 1978); *The Encyclopedia of How It Works, From Abacus to Zoom Lens* (A & W, 1977). De Bono, Edward, ed., *Eureka! An Illustrated History of Inventions From the Wheel to the Computer* (Holt, Rinehart, and Winston, 1974). Farlow, Susan, *Made in America* (Hastings House, 1979). Ferretti, Fred, *The Great American Marble Book* (Workman, 1973). Hooper, Meredith, *Everyday Inventions* (Taplinger, 1976). Houck, Carter, and Parker, Nancy Winslow, *Warm as Wool, Cool as Cotton* (The Seabury Press, 1975). Kaufman, Joe, *What Makes it Go? What Makes it Work? What Makes it Fly? What Makes it Float?* (Western, 1971). Lodewijk, T., *The Way Things Work: An Illustrated Encyclopedia of Technology* (Simon and Schuster, 1973). Mitchell, James, ed., *The Random House Encyclopedia* (Random House, 1977). National Geographic Society, *The Craftsman in America* (1975); *Those Inventive Americans* (1971). Paton, John, ed., *Rand McNally's Children's Encyclopedia of Science* (Rand McNally & Company, 1977). Sarnoff, Jane, and Ruffins, Reynold, *A Great Bicycle Book* (Charles Scribner's Sons, 1973).

CONSULTANTS

Dr. Glenn O. Blough, *Educational Consultant*
Dr. Bernard S. Finn, *Technical Consultant*
Dr. Nicholas J. Long, *Consulting Psychologist*

The Special Publications and School Services Division is grateful to the individuals, organizations, and agencies named in the text and to the individuals cited here for their generous assistance: Rita Adrosko, Smithsonian Institution; Jane May Battaglia, Lever Brothers Company; Don H. Berkebile, Smithsonian Institution; Ken Bostrom, Schwinn Bicycle Company; D. D. Bronikowski, Diamond International Corporation; Ron Campbell, Revell, Inc.; Capitol Contact Lenses, Inc.; Dr. John Conkling, American Pyrotechnics Association; David R. Crippen, Ford Archives/Henry Ford Museum, Dearborn, Michigan; James Dick, R. Dakin & Company; John Dohanic, Steven Manufacturing Company; Richard H. Dowhan and R. M. Rhines, GTE Lighting Products; Earl Dunn and Lamar Newkirk, Georgia-Pacific Corporation; Lucky Elliot, Charles Houston Community Center, Alexandria, Virginia; Eugene C. Gadaire, D.D.S.; Craddock R. Goins, Smithsonian Institution; Donna Grucci and James Grucci, New York Pyrotechnic Products Co., Inc.; Judy Hobart, Librarian; Roger Howdyshell, Marble King, Inc.; Harvey P. Ingalls, J. deBeer & Son, Inc.; R. T. Jagger, The Kendall Company; Dr. Ray Kondratas, Smithsonian Institution; Shirley LaDuke, Little Brownie Bakers; William D. Mellon, Jr., Boeing Commercial Airplane Co.; Larry R. Neuman, Arrow Development Company, Inc.; Kim Payne, Hershey Chocolate Company; Alice S. Rivoire, Girl Scouts of the U.S.A.; Helen L. Smith, Oregon Freeze Dry Foods, Inc.; Ralph Sommariva, State of California Department of Transportation; Carlene Stephens, Smithsonian Institution; Wally Stirling, Burton-Parsons & Company; Robert H. Terranova, The Gillette Company; Reed Trask, Texas Instruments Inc.; Helen Warner, Fenton Art Glass Company; Robert H. Whitman, MacAndrews & Forbes Company; Carolyn Zelle, Pendleton Woolen Mills.

Art on page 21 and on page 56 adapted from *The World Book Encyclopedia*. Copyright © 1980, World Book-Childcraft International, Inc.

Art on page 49 adapted from *Rand McNally's Children's Encyclopedia of Science*. Copyright © 1977, Grisewood & Dempsey Ltd., London.

Illustration on page 100 reproduced from *Electro Type Specimens*. With permission of Morgan & Morgan, Inc.

HOW THINGS ARE MADE

PUBLISHED BY
THE NATIONAL GEOGRAPHIC SOCIETY
WASHINGTON, D. C.

Gilbert M. Grosvenor, *President*
Melvin M. Payne, *Chairman of the Board*
Owen R. Anderson, *Executive Vice President*
Robert L. Breeden, *Vice President, Publications and Educational Media*

PREPARED BY THE SPECIAL PUBLICATIONS
AND SCHOOL SERVICES DIVISION

Donald J. Crump, *Director*
Philip B. Silcott, *Associate Director*
William L. Allen, William R. Gray, *Assistant Directors*

STAFF FOR BOOKS FOR WORLD EXPLORERS SERIES: Ralph Gray, *Editor;* Pat Robbins, *Managing Editor;* Ursula Perrin Vosseler, *Art Director*

STAFF FOR HOW THINGS ARE MADE: Paul D. Martin, *Managing Editor;* Charles E. Herron, Alison Wilbur, *Picture Editors;* Ursula Perrin Vosseler, *Designer;* Lynette Ruschak, *Assistant Designer;* Mary B. Campbell, Penelope Diamanti de Widt, Mary Lee Elden, Libby Parker, *Researchers;* Liza Carter, *Research Assistant*

WRITERS: Arnold B. Ajello (Bridges), Alice Berman (Paper), Jan Leslie Cook (Plastic Models, Fireplace Tools, Matches, Jewelry), James A. Cox (Bicycles, Kaleidoscopes), Susan Farlow (Factory Tours), Marilyn Fenichel (Wool Cloth), Andrea Fisher (Marbles, Tiny Furniture), Patricia C. Hass (Jumbo Jets), David A. Hounshell (Manufacturing Through the Ages), Karin Kinney (Stuffed Animals, Stick-on Bandages), Margaret McKelway (Light Bulbs), Peter E. Muller (Freeze-dried Food, Watches, Grandfather Clocks), Catherine O'Neill (Toothpaste, Felt-tip Markers, Cookies, Contact Lenses, Section Introductions), Karen N. Skeirik (Baseballs, Fireworks), Sharon W. Walsh (Licorice, Flumes)

ILLUSTRATIONS AND DESIGN: Barbara Gibson, *Artist;* Richard A. Fletcher, Kit Pancoast, *Design Assistants*

FAR-OUT FUN: Roger B. Hirschland, *Text Editor;* Patricia N. Holland, *Project Editor;* Sharon Davis (page 8), Barbara Gibson (pages 2, 10-12, 23), Dan Johnson, Art Direction, Inc. (pages 1, 3-7, 15-18), Lynette Ruschak (pages 20-22), Roz Schanzer (pages 9, 13-14), *Artists*

ENGRAVING, PRINTING, AND PRODUCT MANUFACTURE: Robert W. Messer, *Manager;* George V. White, *Production Manager;* Gregory Storer, *Production Project Manager;* Mark R. Dunlevy, Richard A. McClure, Raja D. Murshed, Christine A. Roberts, David V. Showers, *Assistant Production Managers;* Susan M. Oehler, *Production Staff Assistant*

STAFF ASSISTANTS: Debra A. Antonini, Pamela A. Black, Barbara Bricks, Jane H. Buxton, Mary Elizabeth Davis, Rosamund Garner, Victoria D. Garrett, Nancy J. Harvey, Joan Hurst, Suzanne J. Jacobson, Glover S. Johns III, Artemis S. Lampathakis, Virginia A. McCoy, Merrick P. Murdock, Cleo Petroff, Jane F. Ray, Marcia J. Robinson, Carol A. Rocheleau, Maria A. Sedillo, Katheryn M. Slocum, Phyllis C. Watt

INTERNS: Andrea V. Borden, Amie C. Cox, Margaret J. Tinsley, Nancy P. White

MARKET RESEARCH: Joe Fowler, Patrick Fowler, Karen A. Geiger, Carrla L. Holmes, Meg McElligott, Stephen F. Moss

INDEX: Jolene M. Blozis